CONQUEST
and
VICTORY

Studies in Joshua

By
CARL ARMERDING

MOODY PRESS
CHICAGO

CONTENTS

3

To my
faithful helpmeet
Eva May

CHAPTER ONE

Preparation for Conquest

The call and commission of Joshua typifies God's equipment for Christian victory

THE LITTLE COUNTRY called Palestine, which most of us know as the Holy Land, seems to have an importance out of all proportion to its size and population. But even a casual glance at a map of the Eastern Hemisphere shows that this land occupies a most strategic position, lying, as it does, at the very heart of three great continents which are the homelands of the white, black and yellow races. It has been called "the bridge of nations" because of the use made of it by other nations in both war and commerce. Its chief city, Jerusalem, is the center of interest for Christians, Jews and Muslims. The Psalmist spoke of it as "the joy of the whole earth," and "the city of the great King" (Ps. 48:2).

Because of its commanding position this country has interested more than one potentate. History tells of more than one battle for possession of this land. Even in our own times there are evidences that the rulers of adjacent countries would like to annex it.

It is not unlikely that Satan has an interest in this land and its future. The Lord Jesus referred to him more than once as "the prince of this world." And the Apostle Paul, by the Spirit, calls him "the prince of the power of the air," or, as Darby renders it, "the ruler of the authority of the air" (Eph. 2:2). As such he controls the wicked spirits referred to in Ephesians 6:12 as principalities and powers. Some of these are specifically mentioned in Daniel 10 as "the prince of Persia" and "the prince of Grecia." It was "the prince of the kingdom of Persia" who for three whole weeks withstood the extraordinary being who came in answer to Daniel's prayer. This most certainly indicates that he was a superhuman being.

The fact that "the prince of Persia" is mentioned along with "Michael, one of the chief princes," whom Jude calls "the archangel," gives us further reason to believe that he was something more than an ordinary human prince. When Daniel prayed, he was not wrestling with flesh and blood, but with supernatural powers. And every Christian who would really possess the possessions with which he has been blessed in the heavenlies (Eph. 1:3) must face the same foes and fight the same fight.

CANAAN A TYPE OF SPIRITUAL WARFARE

It is of such conflicts that the book of Joshua gives us illustrations and types. The land of Canaan where these battles were fought is a type, not of heaven itself but rather of the heavenly places mentioned in the Epistle to the Ephesians.

A distinction needs to be made between heaven and the heavenly places, for the heavenly places are a scene of conflict, and not of peace and rest. The conflict is with wicked spirits and the rulers of this world's darkness. The nations of Canaan are types of these principalities and powers. The human kings and princes were but the puppets of these powers.

Because this is so we may learn some very important lessons from a study of the book of Joshua which will help us in our spiritual warfare with the supernatural forces which infest the heavenlies. When we really pray and "come boldly to the throne of grace" we are actually invading the domain of the prince of the power of the air. For that reason we need to have on the whole armor of God.

But we need have no fear on that account, for greater is He that is in us than he that is in the world. The same One who indwelt and empowered men of faith in other days will enable us to prevail, even as they did. Satan and his host will contest every bit of progress we may make, but through Him who loved us we shall be more than conquerors. With this in mind, let us proceed with our study.

It is quite possible that Joshua and the Israelites were somewhat disheartened by the death of Moses. Perhaps some were saying, "Moses is dead. We shall never see another man like him. What shall we do now that Moses is dead?" Similar questions and statements are heard whenever some great spiritual leader is taken from us. Israel would have good reason to be disheartened, for Moses was a great man and a great leader. But his death was no untimely accident. From the time that he smote the rock in Kadesh, instead of speaking to it as he had been commanded, he knew that he was not going to bring the children of Israel into the land of promise. Therefore, the nearer they got to the border of their inheritance the nearer he drew to the end of his life.

But the Lord had actually appointed and named his successor long before. Moses himself said that he was told to "charge Joshua, and encourage him, and strengthen him: for he shall go over before this people, and he shall cause them to inherit the land" (Deut. 3:28).

Moses had really prayed for such a successor. Said he, "Let the Lord, the God of the spirits of all flesh, set a man over the congregation, which may go out before them, and which may go in before them, and which may lead them out, and which may

bring them in; that the congregation of the LORD
be not as sheep which have no shepherd" (Num.
27:16-17). Joshua was the answer to that prayer.
And he "was full of the spirit of wisdom; for Moses
had laid his hands upon him" (Deut. 34:9).

This marked a turning point in the history of
Israel. Under the leadership of Joshua they began
a new epoch in their career as a nation. How much
they would have lost if they had refused to go on
because Moses was dead!

In Egypt they had grown from one family into a
nation. In the wilderness, as a nation, they experienced both the goodness and the severity of God.
Now they were about to realize the fulfillment of the
promises made to their fathers centuries before.

But there was to be hard fighting ahead. In Egypt
they endured hard bondage under the tyranny of
Pharaoh. In the wilderness they had fought with
Amalek and other foes. But in Canaan they were to
face an entirely different kind of warfare. In Egypt
they had to be submissive; in the wilderness they
were mostly on the defensive; but now they were
to take the offensive. They did not come into Canaan
as visitors nor as pilgrims. They came as invaders,
with divine orders to conquer and to destroy the
inhabitants of the land, and then to take possession.

WHY THE CANAANITES WERE DESTROYED

The reason for destroying the Canaanites may not
be apparent to some at first sight. It seems unfair
that nations that had lived there so long should be
dispossessed and destroyed. To say the least, such
dispossession looks like unjust interference with the
sovereign rights of others. But when we turn back
the pages of history we find that the Canaanites had
forfeited their right to live anywhere.

When the Lord first promised this land to Abraham and to his descendants, these nations were living undisturbed in their wickedness and idolatry. A jealous God might have used that as His justification for their destruction then and there. But He is long-suffering. And so He informed His servant Abraham that even though He had promised him the land, his immediate descendants were to live as exiles in a land not theirs, and that they were to endure affliction and bondage there. But after that, so he was told, they would depart from that land with great substance.

In the meantime, the inhabitants of Canaan would be given years of grace because "the iniquity of the Amorites" was not yet full (Gen. 15:16). In those years they demonstrated that they were utterly corrupt, until the land itself vomited out its inhabitants (Lev. 18:25).

Such was the state of affairs when Joshua and the Israelites arrived on the east side of the Jordan river. The judgment of God, long deferred, was about to fall. Even so, it did not come without warning. The destruction of Sodom and Gomorrah, in the days of Abraham, was such a warning, had they cared to heed it.

The very presence of Abraham in their midst must have been a testimony in itself. His godly, consecrated life and worship of the true and living God must have been like a light shining in a dark place. That the Canaanites knew something of Abraham's worth and his faith was manifested at the time of Sarah's death. At that time he was recognized as "a mighty prince" even though he claimed to be only "a stranger and a sojourner" (Gen. 23:4).

Abraham's great contemporary, Melchizedek, was at that time king of Salem as well as a priest of the Most High God. He was another whose life and testimony must have been known to all in those parts. Therefore we conclude that the Canaanites were without excuse. They despised the riches of God's "goodness and forbearance and longsuffering" (Rom. 2:4). Therefore He poured out His wrath upon them. When His own people fell into idolatry and unholy practices, God showed that He is no respecter of persons. It was He who delivered them into the hands of the Assyrians because they were no longer worthy to reside in "the glory of all lands."

GOD'S DEALINGS WITH MOSES

The death of Moses, referred to in the opening verse of the book of Joshua, is further proof of God's impartiality. Moses was not permitted to conduct the people across the Jordan, nor to enter the land, because he and his brother Aaron trespassed against Jehovah at the waters of Meribah (Deut. 32:51). Moses was permitted to see the land from the top of Mount Nebo in the land of Moab, but that was as far as he was allowed to go at that time. His death, therefore, would be a solemn reminder to all Israel that even so prominent a leader as Moses was not exempt from the divine discipline when necessary.

Nevertheless, the repeated references to Moses which we find here show how highly God esteemed his services as a leader of His people. Not only does he call Moses "the servant of the Lord" but He also affectionately refers to him as "My servant."

Moses was the one through whom the Lord made known His mind at that time. "He made known His ways unto Moses" (Ps. 103:7). Therefore we hear God saying, "As I said unto Moses." He was one to whom and through whom God could speak. God could have spoken to His people directly, but He chose Moses as a mediator (Gal. 3:19; John 1:17). The Lord could also have led His people in person.

As a matter of fact, He did lead them in person, as we shall see when we come to study Joshua 5:13-15. But He also chose to work through a human leader.

And so, even before the death of Moses, God designated His choice of "Joshua the son of Nun, Moses' minister." In the closing chapter of this book Joshua is also called "the servant of the Lord." But here he is called Moses' attendant. That gave him a distinct connection with the great leader of the past and also implied that he had the necessary training and experience to be Moses' successor.

JOSHUA'S EARLY HISTORY

Joshua was no novice. Having learned to obey, he was qualified to command. He was old enough to have been born in Egypt. Therefore he must have known from experience all about the Passover and the crossing of the Red Sea. From the genealogy given in I Chronicles 7:27 we gather that he was the eldest son of his father. As such he would have a very special interest in the sprinkling of the blood of the paschal lamb.

The first biblical notice of Joshua occurs in Exodus 17. There we read that Moses commissioned him to recruit the forces necessary to fight Amalek. He proved himself as a good soldier when he broke the power of Amalek and his people with the edge of the sword. It was at that time that the Lord said unto Moses, "Write this for a memorial in a book, and rehearse it in the ears of Joshua: for I will utterly put out the remembrance of Amalek from under heaven."

It may be that this very experience gave Joshua the courage that he, together with Caleb, displayed later at Kadesh. It was part of his training as Moses' minister. The way to greatness is ever through service. The Lord Jesus said, "Whosoever will be great

among you, let him be your minister [lit., deacon];
and whosoever will be chief among you, let him be
your servant [lit., slave]" (Matt. 20:26-27).

It was Moses who first called him Joshua. His
original name was Hoshea, which means "deliverance." Moses added a prefix to that and called him
Jehoshua (Num. 13:16). In this form the name has
the same meaning as the blessed name of Jesus.

Joshua was a prince of the tribe of Ephraim and
one of the twelve spies sent by Moses from the
wilderness of Paran to search out the land of
Canaan. When the spies returned from this mission,
Joshua and Caleb urged the immediate conquest of
the land. But the only response they got was that
"all the congregation bade stone them with stones."
It was only by divine intervention that their lives
were saved at that time. Thus Joshua was preserved
for the work he was destined to do, a prophecy of
which may be read in the meaning of his name.

AN EXHIBIT OF GOD'S GRACE

Joshua was also "the son of Nun," a fact which
is repeated again and again in this book. A study
of his genealogy (I Chron. 7:20-28) leads to the
discovery that some of his relatives did not have a
very good reputation. They were cattle thieves. Now,
we call attention to this not because we wish in any
wise to defame the character of this noble man but
rather that we may magnify the sovereign grace of
God.

The sons of Ephraim who brought the family into
disrepute constituted what may be called a "first
family." They were slain by the men of Gath because they came down to take their cattle. After
mourning for them many days, the Lord gave
Ephraim a second family. The firstborn of this
family was Beriah, so named because "he was born

when calamity was in his house." No doubt all of this had some effect on the character of Joshua, otherwise the Spirit of God would not have caused it to be recorded in His word.

Even though Moses had laid his hands upon Joshua, and he was filled with the spirit of wisdom, it was not until after the death of Moses that Joshua was promoted. After that, his leadership was never disputed. Nevertheless, like many another suddenly put into a position of great responsibility, he needed encouragement.

We gather from what follows here that Joshua did not accept this position lightly, nor in self-confidence. Evidently he was a humble man who valued the divine encouragement which he received. It was the Lord Himself who encouraged him, saying, "Now therefore arise, go over this Jordan, thou, and all this people, unto the land which I do give to them, even to the children of Israel." Stephen, in his "apology," referred to this land as "the possession of the Gentiles, whom God drave out before the face of our fathers" (Acts 7:45).

GOD A LOVING GIVER

The thing that is emphasized in Joshua 1 is the fact that this land was God's *gift* to His people. He called it "the land which I do give to them" (v. 2). "Every place that the sole of your foot shall tread upon, that have I *given* unto you" (v. 3). And again, in verse 6, He said, "the land, which I sware unto their fathers to *give* them" (see also vv. 11, 13, 15). Thus did the Lord impress upon Joshua the fact that He was the giver of this land.

The spring of God's generosity is His love. "Because he loved thy fathers, therefore he chose their seed after them, and brought thee out in his sight with his mighty power out of Egypt; to drive out the nations from before thee greater and mightier than thou art, to bring thee in, to give thee their land for an inheritance, as it is this day" (Deut. 4:37-38). Moreover He bound Himself with an oath to do this. That made it irrevocable.

But God does not present His gifts to the unwilling, neither does He bestow them upon a lazy soul. When He said, "Every place that the sole of your foot shall tread upon, that have I given you," He meant that they must go in and take possession. Only in this way could they prove the goodness of God. Those who refused to enter at Kadesh never possessed the land. "The word preached did not profit them, not being mixed with faith in them that heard it" (Heb. 4:2).

This is intended as a word of warning to us. "Let us labor therefore to enter into that rest, lest any man fall after the same example of unbelief" (Heb. 4:11).

Wonderful possibilities were set before the Israelites. The vastness of God's gift to them is indicated in the words: "From the wilderness and this Lebanon even unto the great river, the river Euphrates, all the land of the Hittites, and unto the great sea toward the going down of the sun, shall be your coast" (Joshua 1:4).

These words give us a comprehensive and interesting description of their future inheritance. Those inhabiting the land at that time were to learn that the God of Israel is the Lord of all the earth (Joshua 3:11). As we have seen, He was fully justified in expelling them. On the other hand, He did not give the land to Israel unconditionally. If, like the Gentiles, they too should lapse into idolatry and all that that would involve, then they also would perish from off the land and be scattered among the nations (Deut. 4:26-27).

When God gives, He gives generously. The country we are considering may be small as compared with other lands, but it has great boundaries, and great possibilities. From the *great* wilderness on the south, to the *great* Lebanon on the north, to the *great* river Euphrates on the east, to the *great* sea on the west, was to be their coast, or boundary. As another has pointed out, a country with such boundaries is bound to be great even though it be small geographically. Its greatness is to be measured not in square miles but in strategic importance. But the thing that makes this land truly great is the fact that there our blessed Lord lived and died and rose again in order that we might have an inheritance incorruptible and undefiled, and that fadeth not away (I Peter 1:4).

God not only promised His people all of this land but He confirmed His promise with an oath when He swore unto their fathers that He would give it unto them. Since the gifts and calling of God are without repentance on His part, the promise is irrevocable. Its immutability is inseparably linked up with His faithfulness. "*As* I was with Moses, *so* I will be with thee."

He changes not! Men may come and men may go, but He abideth faithful. It must have been a great encouragement to Joshua when he was assured by the Lord Himself that He would be with him even as He had been with Moses. And because of this Joshua was to be invincible! "There shall not a man be able to stand before thee all the days of thy life." With the single exception of the temporary defeat at Ai, he went from victory to victory, a most amazing record.

This should be an encouragement to us. Our Lord has promised us His personal presence no less than He promised it to Joshua (Matt. 28:19). Moreover, He has given us His Holy Spirit, who is to abide with us for ever (John 14:16). Therefore we need have no fear, because greater is He that is in us than he that is in the world (I John 4:4). Thus we are assured of victory in our conflict with satanic powers. We are more than conquerors through Him that loved us (Rom. 8:37).

CHAPTER TWO

Be Strong and of Good Courage

(Joshua 1:6-18)

THE GRAND PURPOSE of all God's dealings with us is
that we may come to know Him. Our Lord Jesus
said, "This is life eternal, that they might know thee
the only true God, and Jesus Christ, whom thou
has sent" (John 17:3).

Joshua knew Him as a loving God who bestows
His gifts apart altogether from human merit (Deut.
4:37). He had come to know Him as a generous
God who, even though He set bounds to the promised inheritance, made them great bounds which
would encourage the believing soul to go in and take
possession. God had also revealed Himself as the
faithful God who changes not. But now Joshua was
to know Him also as the God of all encouragement
(II Cor. 1:3).

Thus far all had been one-sided, so to speak. The
Lord had confirmed His promise to give Israel the
land. He had further promised that He would neither
leave nor forsake His servant Joshua in his conquest
of that land. But in Joshua 1:6 we see that this involved responsive action on the part of the one to
whom such promises were made. Joshua was told
to be strong and of a good courage because he was
to divide for an inheritance the land which the Lord
had sworn He would give Israel. It was impressed
upon Joshua that he was to serve for the sake of
others, and to cause them to inherit their possessions.

In other words, it was not to be a matter of personal gain or glory. His own reward would come later.

Such altruism and unselfishness should characterize every servant of the Lord. We recall that after the Lord had blessed the loaves and fishes He gave them to His disciples that they might first feed others. The fragments left over would more than meet their personal needs later. The faithful servant is made ruler over the household, not that he may lord it over that household, but in order that he may give them meat in due season (Matt. 24: 45-47).

By nature every one of us is selfish. Only those who are born again can consistently render faithful, unselfish service from the heart. Moreover, such service requires something more than physical strength or natural courage. The enemies which Joshua had to face were human, of course. But the strength and courage necessary to overcome them had to be superhuman. One's weapons may be the very best obtainable, but unless one's heart is in the fight he is not likely to win. And what is courage but heart?

The Lord did not say to Joshua, "Be patriotic and fight for your country and for your people." Devotion to one's country is a wonderful thing. But the good soldier of Jesus Christ must have a motive superior to that. His *strength* must be in the Lord and in the *power* of His *might* (Eph. 6:10). It is quite remarkable to find three such closely related words in one verse. But the source of all three is "in the Lord." And it is interesting to observe that they occur in a passage which we believe finds its illustration in the book of Joshua. The nations of Canaan are types of the principalities mentioned in Ephesians 6:12.

THE DIFFICULTIES OF LEADERSHIP

Three times the Lord encouraged Joshua to be strong and of a good courage. And each time he encouraged him He also gave him good reason to be courageous. This is indicated by the occurrence of the little word "for" in verses 6, 8, and 9.

In verse 6 we read, "*For* unto this people shalt thou divide for an inheritance the land." A more accurate translation reads, "For thou shalt cause this people to inherit the land." That was no easy task. Joshua knew from his experience at Kadesh-barnea how difficult it is to get people to go in and possess their possessions.

Similar difficulties face the servant of Christ today as he seeks to lead the people of God into their spiritual inheritance. For example, it is almost impossible to get some Christians to accept the teaching found in the epistles to the Romans and to the Galatians, that we are "not under the law, but under grace" (Rom. 6:14). Some refuse to believe that a sheep of Christ can never perish (John 10:28). Others, when they see that the enjoyment of their spiritual possessions involves a struggle with Satan and his hosts, are content to remain in the wilderness, as it were, so far as progress in divine things is concerned. Such generally excuse themselves by saying that they are quite content with "the simple gospel."

For a babe in Christ to desire milk is normal (I Peter 2:2). But for one who has known the Lord for years to need a milk diet would be a mark of carnality and not of spirituality (I Cor. 3:1-3). It was to such that the apostle had to write, "We have many things to say, and hard to be uttered, seeing ye are dull of hearing. For when for the time ye

ought to be teachers, ye have need that one teach
you again which be the first principles of the oracles
of God; and are become such as have need of milk,
and not of strong meat. For every one that useth
milk is unskilful in the word of righteousness: for
he is a babe. But strong meat belongeth to them that
are of full age, even to those who by reason of use
have their senses exercised to discern both good and
evil" (Heb. 5:11-14). Indeed, it does take courage
for some to inherit what God has so graciously given
them.

THE COURAGE TO DEAL WITH SELF

The Lord's second exhortation to Joshua, found
in Joshua 1:7, is somewhat stronger than the first,
and it is also more personal. The context gives us
the reason for this difference. It always takes more
courage to deal with self than it does to deal with
others. Every true servant of Christ knows that from
personal experience. It is easier to exhort others to
be obedient to the whole Word of God than it is
to be completely obedient ourselves. Therefore He
says to His servant, "Only be thou strong and very
courageous, that thou mayest observe to do according to all the law, which Moses my servant commanded thee."

This fresh reference to Moses is very interesting
and instructive. It may have been a "new day" for
Joshua, but God did not give him any new rules
or standards of conduct. The old standards remained, they were not out of date. There are those
who think that a change is in order simply because
times have changed. But God's moral standards are
timeless. He did not command His people to be holy
because holiness suited the times and circumstances
in which they lived. He said, "Ye shall be holy; for
I am holy" (Lev. 11:44; I Peter 1:16).

In saying this we are not unmindful of the fact that

dispensations differ. To be under the law is one thing; to be under grace is quite another. But when Joshua and the Israelites arrived in Canaan they were no less under the law than when they were at Sinai. There had been no change of dispensation meanwhile. Neither has there been any change of dispensation since the principles which are to govern us were laid down by the Lord and His apostles.

OBEDIENCE TO THE SPIRIT OF THE LAW

It was not only the letter of the law that Joshua was to observe. He was "to do *according* to all the law." And one who does *according* to the Word of God does not require a special text for every detail of his conduct. Questions whether one may go here or there, or do this or that, find their answer in the spirit of Scripture as well as in the letter. This principle is recognized everywhere. Even men of the world talk about the spirit, or intent, of the law, as distinguished from its letter.

Joshua's obedience to the law was to be complete, according to *all* the law. He had no choice or preference in the matter. "All scripture is given by inspiration of God, and is profitable for doctrine, for reproof, for correction, for instruction in righteousness: that the man of God may be perfect, throughly furnished unto all good works (II Tim. 3:16-17).

Finally, Joshua's obedience was to be consistent. The Lord commanded His servant to take a straight course, turning neither to the right hand nor the left. He was to allow himself no latitude, as some would say. In so doing he would not waste precious energy in weaving from side to side of the road. If this world is, as it should be, nothing but "a wilderness wide," we need not make many side trips to see the scenery. Let us rather make straight paths for our feet (Heb. 12:13). Alas, many of the professed children of God find the straight paths too confining and uninteresting. But if we would prosper spiritually, we must give to the Word of God constant, consistent, and complete obedience.

It is not enough to obey "up to a point," as though it were left to us to decide how much or how little of the Word we should obey when it clearly applies to us. We have the assurance of the Lord Jesus Himself that if any man willeth to do His will he shall know of the doctrine (John 7:17). The same grace that brings us salvation also teaches us to live soberly, righteously, and godly in this present world (Titus 2:12). This kind of obedience should characterize all who aspire to leadership among the people of God. It is to such that He promises "good success."

FAMILIARITY WITH THE SCRIPTURES

The method by which all of this is achieved is clearly stated in verse 8. The book of the law was not to depart out of Joshua's mouth. He was to talk the language of Scripture. How suitable are its "right words" for every occasion and in every place! Whether one be called upon to speak to kings or to peasants, his language, if biblical, will always be fitting.

Let us not waste our time trying to acquire the speech of a world which is constantly inventing some new slang in its vain attempt to give zest and force to what is being said. The effectiveness of simple speech such as one finds in the Bible needs no such doubtful improvements.

Nothing is more desirable for the minister of the Word of God than to be steeped in the very diction and style of the Bible. Of course, this will require something more than a casual or hasty reading of it. One must meditate in God's Word day and night.

One must delight in it. The psalmist said, "O how I love thy law! it is my meditation all the day." He also said, "How sweet are thy words unto my taste! yea, sweeter than honey to my mouth" (Ps. 119:97, 103)!

To meditate on the Word of God means to digest it. As we feed upon the Word and digest it, it becomes part of us. Then obedience to it becomes intuitive, and spiritual success and prosperity will surely follow.

Again the Lord exhorts Joshua to "be strong and of a good courage" (v. 9). But this time His exhortation is preceded by the question, "Have not I commanded thee?" The Lord had just referred to the commandment of Moses. But here we learn that it was really His commandment. Moses was but His mouthpiece. That gave his utterances divine authority. In the same way, the words of an apostle, given by inspiration of God, have the same authority as the words of the Lord Jesus Himself. See I Corinthians 14:37. Joshua had to learn that it was not man who had commanded him to be strong and courageous. It was the Lord Himself.

But then the Lord added what Moses could not say: "For the LORD thy God is with thee whithersoever thou goest" (v. 9). This promise is the best of all reasons for being strong and courageous. Moses knew the value of God's presence. Without it he would not move (Exodus 33:12-16). It was he who said, "Wherein shall it be known here that I and thy people have found grace in thy sight? is it not in that thou goest with us? so shall we be separated [distinguished], I and thy people, from all the people that are upon the face of the earth."

Because of this same blessed Presence the psalmist was unafraid as he walked through the valley of deathly gloom. And this same Presence is promised to us. Before our Lord ascended to heaven, He assured His disciples that He would be with them all the days, even to the end of the age.

THE CERTAINTY OF VICTORY

It is remarkable that little or nothing is said about the enemies Joshua would have to meet. They are referred to quite incidentally, and Joshua was assured that not one of them would be able to stand before him all the days of his life. Therefore he had no reason to be afraid or dismayed.

We all know that fear and dismay are often the worst enemies we have. But we notice that the Lord constantly kept the eyes and mind of His servant fixed on the goal—the possession of the land and the enjoyment of the inheritance.

Both Joshua and Caleb had their hearts set on the land flowing with milk and honey while their brethren worried about the wicked inhabitants of the land and the giants that lived there. The spies who accompanied Caleb and Joshua had to admit that it was a good land. They said, "We came unto the land . . . , and surely it floweth with milk and honey; and this is the fruit of it" (Num. 13:27). But they turned right around and contradicted all that by saying, "The land, through which we have gone to search it, is a land that eateth up the inhabitants thereof; and all the people that we saw in it are men of great stature" (v. 32).

Just how any country could produce men of great stature and at the same time consume its inhabitants is a bit difficult to understand. But such are the arguments of unbelief, with its accompanying pessimism and discouragement. In the first chapter of Joshua, however, we hear none of this. The Lord had commanded him! Was not that enough? It certainly was.

The prediction that he was to divide the land for an inheritance carried with it the guarantee of victorious conquest. One cannot divide that which he does not possess. Oh, that we were as ready to take the Lord at His word as Joshua was!

Joshua began his career as Moses' minister, and then became his successor. But his task was quite different from that of Moses. To lead the people across the desert was one thing. To lead them into battle against nations who would dispute every bit of progress was quite another. Hence God gave special encouragements to Joshua.

INITIAL PLANS FOR CONQUEST

Immediately after being divinely commissioned Joshua took command. We read, in verses 10 and 11, that he commanded "the officers of the people, saying, Pass through the host, and command the people, saying, Prepare you victuals; for within three days ye shall pass over this Jordan, to go in to possess the land, which the LORD your God giveth you to possess it."

True leader that he was, Joshua knew how to assign certain tasks to others. He could have given the command direct to the people. But he showed his qualifications for leadership when he "commanded the officers of the people" to do that. In a somewhat similar way our Lord worked through His disciples in meeting the need of the multitude in feeding them with the loaves and fishes. In Joshua, of course, the people were told to prepare themselves victuals. Nevertheless there is enough similarity to warrant a comparison. Like the Lord Jesus, Joshua was concerned about the need of the people. Before they left Egypt they had eaten the lamb, roasted with fire, and unleavened bread. They ate in haste, with loins girded and staff in hand. The people under

Joshua felt no immediate need of haste. Within
three days they were to pass over the Jordan.

This apparent delay of three days may look like
a waste of time. But we shall learn later what took
place during those three days. These were days of
waiting and of preparation for the nation as a whole.
For the city of Jericho they were days of grace, even
though only one household availed itself of that
grace. Thus we can see that there were reasons for
this apparent delay.

A most remarkable thing about these days of
preparation is the fact that nothing was said about
Israel's enemies, nor the weapons they would need
to fight them. Ever and always it was the promised
possession which was kept before them.

THE UNITY OF GOD'S PEOPLE

It was during this time of waiting and preparation
that Joshua had a special word for the two and a
half tribes which had already entered into their
possession east of the Jordan. The Lord had given
them rest and He had given them that land. Joshua
reminded them of what Moses had commanded
them when he, under God, gave them the land. They
were not to settle down there as those who had
arrived, while their brethren went on to fight for their
possession on the west of Jordan. Accordingly all
of their valiant men were commanded to go over
before their brethren "until the LORD have given
your brethren rest, as he hath given you, and they
also have possessed the land which the LORD your
God giveth them" (1:15).

As a nation the Israelites were a unit, even though
they had their tribal divisions. They were to manifest their unity in presenting a united front against
their common foes. In this they may serve as an
illustration for the Church, especially in these days

when there is so much dissension, and even strife, among the Lord's people. The ecumenical movement is an attempt to overcome divisions among Christians, but there is a vast difference between union and unity. Man may achieve the former; only the Holy Spirit can effect the latter. "By one Spirit are we all baptized into one body, whether we be Jews or Gentiles, whether bond or free; and have all been made to drink into one Spirit" (I Cor. 12:13). We are told to endeavor "to keep the unity of the Spirit in the bond of peace" (Eph. 4:3). But all such endeavor must be consistent with the truth as revealed in the Word of God.

Israel's response to Joshua's command is inspiring. Not only did they promise complete obedience, but they also promised their obedience was to be of the same quality as that rendered to his great predecessor Moses. Yea, they went even further in promising that any one who rebelled against the commands of Joshua was to be put to death. Insubordination would not be tolerated. And it is rather striking that the people themselves decided what the penalty was to be. And then, just as if they had heard the Lord speaking to Joshua, they repeated the divine encouragement, "Be strong and of a good courage."

What more could any leader ask? And, so far as the record goes, they never lost that spirit of devotion to Joshua. We do not read that they ever rebelled against his authority. Therefore, when Joshua "mustered out" these men (Joshua 22) he did so with words of commendation and blessing, words that were a testimony to their faithfulness. And what an example for us! The Lord help us to be like-minded in unswerving obedience and loyalty to the Captain of our salvation. And let us consider it a privilege to have a part in the great work of causing others to inherit and enjoy the blessings which are theirs and ours in Christ.

CHAPTER THREE

Reconnaissance at Jericho

(Joshua 2)

BEFORE THE ACTUAL INVASION and conquest of
Canaan, there was a brief pause while a survey was
made of what was probably the chief city in the land
at that time. This brief respite is quite in keeping
with the ways of God as seen elsewhere in Scripture.
Before the Lord expelled Adam and Eve from the
Garden of Eden, He came down to talk with Adam
concerning his sin. He did likewise before He pronounced judgment on Cain. Before He brought the
flood upon the earth in the days of Noah, there was
a waiting period while the ark was being built.

Before God confounded the languages of men at
Babel, He "came down to see the city and the tower,
which the children of men builded" (Gen. 11:5).
Likewise, before He destroyed Sodom and Gomorrah, He paused before smiting in judgment. Judgment is His "strange work" (Isa. 28:21).

He did not drive out the Canaanite in the days
of Abraham because the iniquity of the Amorites
was not yet full (Gen. 15:16). But evidently it had
reached its fullness by this time, and the prediction
that Abraham's seed was to come into the land again
in the fourth generation was about to be fulfilled.
But the God of all grace still lingered over a scene
that was fully ripe for judgment. Truly He is long-
suffering and patient!

The secret mission of the spies whom Joshua sent

had two objectives. Its primary purpose was to "view the land, even Jericho." But it was also to extend mercy to Rahab, whose sinful life had put her among the worst of sinners. The sovereign grace of God never stood out in bolder relief than it did when He sent His two servants to the house of Rahab. But the moment it became evident that our gracious God had an interest in a soul like that, the enemy got busy and tried to prevent, if possible, the work of salvation.

We have already seen that the kings of Canaan are types of the principalities and powers mentioned in Ephesians 6:12. The fact that the king of Jericho was the first of these to be dealt with gives him an importance which makes it appear that he may be a type of the devil himself, whom the Lord Jesus called "the prince of this world."

The fact that Jericho lay just north of the ruins of Sodom and Gomorrah makes it reasonably certain that the king of Jericho knew of the judgment which overtook those cities because of their wickedness. In any case, he was hostile to the people of God. His "intelligence department" had evidently brought him the news that men had come in that night from the children of Israel to search out the land. Thus he was made aware of the latest plans of the host of Israel.

In the same way our enemy, the devil, seems to know almost immediately about any move to be made by the servants of the Lord. As long as men live in sin and pagan darkness, he seems not to care whether a country is open or closed to the outside world. But the moment plans are made to send missionaries to such a field, all sorts of hindrances arise. And even though missionaries may have been working in a country for years, the enemy frequently succeeds in closing the door against further reinforcements, and even against the return of missionaries who have been on furlough.

Anyone at all acquainted with missionary work knows that this is so. Satan is our untiring opponent. He claims all the kingdoms of the world as his own. Therefore, we never move into any field without being made to feel that we are intruders, to say the least.

CHRISTIANS ARE WATCHED

Then, too, we know that very often the missionary's first converts are somewhat timid about identifying themselves with him because they fear persecution. Like Rahab, after she had received the spies, they will be under surveillance. It is not likely that Rahab received much notice from the king previous to this.

As soon as she had received the messengers, however, she attracted the royal attention. The fact that she lied to the king is not to be wondered at. If the king of Jericho is a type of him who is "a liar and the father of it" (John 8:44), then we need not be surprised if one of his subjects lies to him. It is significant that whenever Rahab is referred to in the New Testament she is never called a liar, even though she is referred to as a harlot. Her lie is never mentioned.

That is not because her sin was overlooked; it was forgiven. But she is still called "the harlot," just as Paul referred to himself as "the chief of sinners." What she *did* was put away forever. What she *was* is mentioned only to magnify the grace that saved her.

It should be noticed that even though Rahab lied to her old master, the king of Jericho, she was strictly honest and truthful with the spies. She was perfectly frank with them even though she knew that

her own life was in jeopardy and that her country
was doomed. She offered no reason why it should
not be destroyed. From some source, not revealed
here, she had learned that God had given the land
to Israel. She never questioned the justice of that,
as some do today. She told the spies that she had
heard that the Lord had dried up the waters of the
Red Sea from before them when they came out of
Egypt. Only forty years had passed since that great
event had taken place. It must have been fresh in
the memory of many then living. And the testimony
of a witness outside of Israel, in a matter like this,
is of great weight.

She had also heard what Israel had done to the
two kings of the Amorites on the other side of Jordan, Sihon and Og, whom they utterly destroyed.
That was much more recent and also a good deal
nearer home. And she did not hesitate to tell the
spies the effect of all this on her people.

It is very evident that every move of the Israelites
was as well known as if there had been a news cor-
respondent on the spot to report each detail. But
the news brought no comfort to the Canaanites. On
the other hand, it must have been an encouragement
to the spies when they heard that terror had fallen
upon the inhabitants of the land because of Israel,
and that there was no more courage in any man because of them.

SATAN FEARS GOD

At Kadesh-barnea it was Israel that feared. Here
it was the Canaanites who were afraid of Israel. And
if we could look behind the scenes into the camp
of those spiritual forces which are arrayed against
us today, we doubtless would see the same. The
devil does not fear us, but he is bound to fear Him
who is in us, for He is greater than he that is in the

world (I John 4:4). Therefore, we need not fear.

However, it was not merely about Israel that Rahab talked, nor yet of what God had done for them. She must have amazed the spies with her knowledge of the Lord Himself. "The LORD your God, he is God in heaven above, and in the earth beneath" (Joshua 2:11). Her words are so similar to those used by our blessed Lord Himself in Matthew 28:18 that we cannot resist the conclusion that she was in reality referring to Him even though she knew Him not.

It is truly remarkable that such words should fall from the lips of a poor benighted Canaanite. With childlike faith she believed the report concerning the drying up of the Red Sea. And she concluded that the One who could do such things must be the Lord of heaven and earth.

The recognition of God's power and sovereignty did not deter her in the least from seeking to know His grace. Her plea for that (v. 12) is very touching. In this she was most unselfish. It was her father's house and her family that she was concerned about first of all. She included herself quite incidentally when she said, "and deliver our lives from death" (v. 13).

Her attitude is somewhat different from that of the Philippian jailer. He was concerned with his personal safety, for he said, "Sirs, what must I do to be saved?" In reply he got more than he asked for. "Believe on the Lord Jesus Christ, and thou shalt be saved, *and thy house*" (Acts 16:31). Rahab reversed the order by pleading first for her father's house. She also was granted her heart's desire, and more.

We have already noticed that the mission of the spies was twofold. This is confirmed by the fact that in the New Testament they are referred to both as "spies" and as "messengers." In Hebrews 11:31 we read, "By faith the harlot Rahab perished not with them that believed not, when she had received the *spies* with peace."

Incidentally, we get a description here of her fellow citizens which is very interesting. They are described as unbelievers. That implies that they, too, had had the opportunity to believe what she did. But they believed not, and because they believed not, they were condemned.

The statements Rahab made to the spies indicate that she was a believer. She believed the report she had heard about the drying up of the Red Sea. And she also believed the report of what had happened nearer home—not very long before the spies arrived at her house. Moreover, she must have known the object of their mission, and yet she received them "with peace."

James, in his epistle, raises the question, "Was not Rahab the harlot justified by works, when she had received the *messengers,* and had sent them out another way?" (James 2:25). He not only used the word "messengers" (lit. "angels") instead of "spies," but he also used a more intense word for "received."

From this we gather that these men went to Jericho not only to survey it and to gather military information but they also went there on an errand of mercy. To Rahab and her household they were "the savour of life unto life," but to the unbelieving they became "the savour of death unto death" (II Cor. 2:16). It has been suggested that we have in these spies, or messengers, a type of the godly remnant of Israel, who in days to come will have a similar ministry to the Gentiles (Isa. 66:19).

Rahab was told not to make their business known after they had left. This agrees with what we know will be the case when those who have had the gospel

preached to them but have rejected it will be denied
the privilege of hearing it again. Because they receive not the love of the truth, that they might be
saved, God will send them a strong delusion and
they will believe the lie; that they all may be judged
who believed not the truth but had pleasure in unrighteousness (cf. II Thess. 2:10-12).

RAHAB PROVED HER FAITH

The scarlet line by which Rahab sent forth the
messengers "another way" was not displayed where
the people of Jericho might see it. It was put in
the window through which she let the men down,
on the outside of the wall. James tells us that in so
doing she gave evidence of the reality of her faith.
Even though he does not actually mention the scarlet line, it is certainly implied in the words "by
another way."

The one thing that is mentioned in both Hebrews
11:31 and James 2:25 is the fact that she *received*
the spies, or the messengers. It so happens that the
Lord commends those on His right hand (see Matthew 25:34-40) for *receiving* "the least of these,"
His brethren. Receiving His brethren is the same as
receiving Him personally. Contrariwise, those who
do not receive His messengers are condemned because they did it not unto Him.

It is remarkable that receiving the messengers is
emphasized in connection with Rahab rather than
hanging the scarlet line in her window. Since the
scarlet line is not actually mentioned in the New
Testament passages which we have just considered,
nor yet in Joshua 6:25, we conclude that the Spirit
of God is emphasizing Rahab's reception of the messengers. In receiving them she received Him who
sent them.

We have a striking parallel to this in the New

Testament. Speaking of the Lord Jesus, John said, "But as many as received him, to them gave he power to become the sons of God, even to them that believe on his name: which were born, not of blood, nor of the will of the flesh, nor of the will of man, but of God" (John 1:12-13). In referring to this verse, we would not set aside the scarlet line and the precious truth which it symbolizes, but we are merely putting the emphasis where the Spirit of God puts it in the passage we are studying.

Having received the messengers, the next thing that Rahab wanted was assurance. "Now therefore," said she, "I pray you, swear unto me by the Lord, since I have showed you kindness, that ye will also show kindness unto my father's house, and give me a true token: and that ye will save alive my father, and my mother, and my brethren, and my sisters, and all that they have, and deliver our lives from death" (Joshua 2:12-13).

She asked for a great deal, but she got all that she asked. And it is remarkable that the spies were able to make promises immediately without having to refer the matter to Joshua. They were ambassadors with full power to act on behalf of their chief. In the same way the Lord Jesus empowered His disciples when He said, "As my Father hath sent me, even so send I you . . . . Whose soever sins ye remit, they are remitted unto them; and whose soever sins ye retain, they are retained" (John 20: 21, 23).

Even before Rahab let the spies down by the rope through the window they told her that they would "deal kindly and truly" with her. This same expression, "kindly and truly," was used by Eleazar (Gen. 24:49) when pleading with Laban and Bethuel for permission to take Rebecca with him to be Isaac's bride. It was also used by Jacob when he made Joseph swear that he would not bury his remains in Egypt (Gen. 47:29).

In dealing "kindly and truly" with Rahab the spies were giving her a foretaste of that "grace and truth" which subsists through Jesus Christ (John 1:17). This incident is another example of those gracious surpluses of which we have a number in Scripture. She asked that the spies would deal "kindly" with her. They gave her more than she asked; they promised to deal both "kindly and truly" with her.

In this we get a good illustration of the way in which the Lord preserves the balance between His love and His righteousness. To deal kindly with one at the expense of truth would not be in keeping with the character of Him who is both light and love.

> 'Tis in the cross of Christ we see,
> How God can save, yet righteous be.

ONLY ONE SAFE PLACE

In that which follows we see what is expected of those who have been dealt with in this way. Rahab had to do two things. She was told, "Thou shalt bind this line of scarlet thread in the window which thou didst let us down by: *and* thou shalt bring thy father, and thy mother, and thy brethren, and all thy father's household, home unto thee" (Joshua 2:18).

To gather the members of her father's household into her house was her task, her responsibility. But those whom she thus gathered must remain in the house (v. 19). In this we see a strong resemblance to the ordinance of the Passover. The binding of the scarlet line in the window answers to the sprinkling of the blood of the lamb on the doorposts. And just as none of the Israelites was to go out of his house until the morning (Exodus 12:22), so all of those who gathered in the house of Rahab had to remain there if they would escape the judgment that was about to fall upon the city.

The only safe place in Jericho just then was Rahab's house. Other houses—not even the king's palace—no matter how beautiful they might be, no matter where they were located, could not give the protection guaranteed to those who would gather in this little home on the town wall. Apparently it was in the most dangerous spot of all. But its safety did not depend upon its location. The scarlet line was its banner of safety, just as the sprinkled blood of the lamb was for the Israelites in Egypt forty years before.

Had Rahab thought only of her own personal safety she might have escaped in the same way that the spies escaped. But she had a service to perform in Jericho which demanded her presence there until the very day that the judgment fell. Thus she was used of the Lord to snatch other souls as brands from the burning.

While all of this was going on inside the city, the hosts of Israel waited on the other side of the Jordan. No doubt some wondered about the outcome of the mission of the spies. But when the spies returned to Joshua they came with a word of complete assurance. "And they said unto Joshua, Truly the Lord hath delivered into our hands *all* the land; for even *all* the inhabitants of the country do faint because of us" (v. 24).

It would have been no small mercy to have escaped from the hands of the king of Jericho after he discovered what they were about. But their escape was something other than a retreat. It was the end of the first stage of the battle of Jericho. Not many days later this stronghold of Satan would be in ruins.

The lesson for us is as simple as it is plain. Satan

may walk about as a roaring lion, seeking whom he may devour. But he is not able to overcome those who resist him steadfastly in the faith. We are more than conquerors through Him that loved us. "But thanks be to God, which giveth us the victory through our Lord Jesus Christ" (I Cor. 15:57).

CHAPTER FOUR

Crossing the Jordan

(Joshua 3)

ONE CANNOT READ this chapter without being impressed by the deliberation with which each move was made. There was no haste. The information brought back by the spies was such that some might have urged an immediate attack on Jericho. The dread of the Israelites had fallen on the Canaanites, and all the inhabitants of the land fainted because of them. But the Israelites did not rush precipitously into battle with the Canaanites.

In order to wage successful and victorious warfare with the Canaanites, the people of the Lord must wait on Him in order to renew their strength. Since "all the children of Israel" are mentioned here we may assume that they were of one mind as to this. Joshua had risen early that morning. Therefore he could hardly be accused of slothfulness in his deliberation. And so they moved from Shittim to the Jordan and lodged there before they passed over.

The Jordan was the last natural barrier that stood between God's people and the promised inheritance. At Kadesh-barnea, where they might have entered some thirty-eight years before, there was no such barrier. With the exception of Caleb and Joshua the generation that had failed to enter then had passed away. A new generation must now learn what their fathers should have learned when they crossed the Red Sea.

The Red Sea and the Jordan are really comple-
mentary in their spiritual significance. The fact that
it took the Israelites forty years to go from the one
to the other is passed over in silence in Psalm 114
where the two are brought together in one verse as
if they were adjacent.

Nevertheless, the crossing of the Jordan was something more than a repetition of the crossing of the
Red Sea. The opening of the one provided a way
out of Egypt; the cutting off of the waters of the
Jordan opened the way into Canaan. In that sense
they were distinct. But the fact remains that if Israel
had entered the land at Kadesh-barnea, there would
have been no need for a second miracle.

But there is no such thing as "skipping grades"
in the school of God. What is not learned at one
time will have to be learned at another. Those who
will not learn from the experiences of a bygone
generation are bound to repeat those experiences for
themselves. And what we learn by personal experience we generally remember.

In a certain sense the crossing of the Jordan was
to be to this generation what the crossing of the
Red Sea had been to their fathers (cf. 4:23-24).
But there was a difference. The older generation
made its exit from a house of bondage. This generation was about to enter a land, the possession of
which must be gained by conquest. Their fathers did
not have to fight their enemies. The waters of the
Red Sea swallowed them up. This generation would
have to fight in order to possess. But whereas the
older generation faced a barren wilderness after their
escape from Egypt, this generation had for its goal
a land flowing with milk and honey.

Then, too, the means used for the opening of a
way through the Red Sea were quite different from
those used for the cutting off of the waters of Jordan.

In the former case, "Moses stretched out his hand over the sea; and the LORD caused the sea to go back by a strong east wind all that night, and made the dry sea land, and the waters were divided" (Exodus 14:21). In making possible the crossing of the Jordan, God did not use a strong wind, but the ark of the covenant was used to open the way. Divine power wrought in both cases, but not in the same way. At the Red Sea God was liberating His redeemed people from the slavery of Egypt. At the Jordan He was giving them access to the land where their possessions lay.

The opening of a passage through the waters of Jordan may be likened to what our Lord did when He ascended on high after He had completed His work on the earth. To ascend where He was before, our Lord had to pass through the domain of the prince of the power of the air, that is, the domain of the devil. "And having spoiled principalities and powers, he made a shew of them openly, triumphing over them in it" (Col. 2:15).

In Psalm 114:3, 5 the Red Sea is said to have *fled,* but the Jordan was *driven,* or turned back. What are we to learn from this difference? Apparently there was powerful opposition in the latter which we do not see in the former. At the Red Sea the Israelites were told to stand still and see the salvation of the Lord. At the Jordan they were told to keep their eyes fixed on the ark of the covenant of the Lord their God.

THREE GREAT TRUTHS

The ark is quite generally considered to be a type of Christ. The fact that it contained the two tables of stone, written with the finger of God, is very suggestive of the One in whose heart the Word of God was so deeply engraved that He could say, "I delight to do thy will, O my God: yea, thy law is within my heart" (Ps. 40:8).

The mercy seat which covered the ark also speaks of Him "whom God hath set forth to be a propitiation, [or, mercy seat] through faith in his blood" (Rom. 3:25). This ark, with the cherubim overshadowing it, was said to be the dwelling place of God (cf. Ps. 80:1). And Colossians 2:9 teaches us that Christ is the One in whom dwells all the fullness of the Godhead bodily.

Thus we may see in the ark three great truths concerning the person of Christ. First, He is the obedient One, who as man walked here below to the glory of God His Father. Second, as the mercy seat, He became the Mediator, the One in whom God and the sinner meet. Third, He is God manifest in flesh, in whom all the fullness of Deity was pleased to dwell.

It was upon this One, in type, that the Israelites were to focus their attention as they prepared to cross the Jordan. At the Red Sea they were told to stand still and see the salvation of the Lord; at the Jordan, though they did not realize the implication of what they were doing, it was the Saviour Himself they were to contemplate.

But they were not only to look upon the ark, they were to go after it. Their fathers before them first had to "stand still" and then to "go forward" (Exodus 14:13, 15). Here, after a pause of three days, they were told to go after the ark (Joshua 3:3). At the Red Sea the angel of the Lord and the pillar of cloud stood behind them to protect them from their pursuers (Exodus 14:19). Here the ark went before them. There was no threat from behind, but much hard fighting ahead.

Their fathers did not have to fight the Egyptians at all. In the wilderness their warfare against such foes as the Amalekites was mostly defensive. But in Canaan, the new generation was to take the offensive, and the Lord Himself would be their Captain. Even though Joshua was their divinely appointed leader, their eyes were not to be upon him, but on the ark, a type of the Lord Himself.

All of this will help us to understand better what follows. There was to be a distance of about two thousand cubits between them and the ark. They were not to come near it so that they might know the way by which they should go. They might have missed their way if they had not observed this rule.

If the ark speaks of our Lord, as we believe it does, then we may see a good reason for this rule. We need ever to remember who and what He is. While it is blessedly true that He has drawn near to us in grace, we must never forget that He is the One who has been exalted "far above all principality, and power, and might, and dominion, and every name that is named, not only in this world, but also in that which is to come" (Eph. 1:21).

Nevertheless, it is our privilege to contemplate His glory with unveiled faces and thus to be transformed into the same image from glory to glory by the Spirit (II Cor. 3:18). The more we do this, the better we shall get to know Him, and the better we shall know the way that He would have us go. And the better we know Him, the more we shall revere and adore Him.

REVERENCE AND INTIMACY

We must not assume that the Israelites had to keep that distance of two thousand cubits because they were not capable of drawing nearer, nor yet because such distance was characteristic of the Old Testament. It is suggestive, rather, of that reverence which is Christ's due no matter how well we may

know Him. We will do well to follow the example
of the disciple who leaned on Christ's bosom, always
addressing Him as Lord. The Lord Jesus Himself
said, "Ye call me Master and Lord: and ye say well;
for so I am" (John 13:13).

Nowhere in Scripture do we read of anyone addressing Him as "brother." Those who know Him
best revere Him most without losing any of their
sense of His nearness and dearness.

In the path of faith we need both a right objective
and a proper perspective. We shall have both if we
give the Lord His rightful place. Then we shall know
the path by which we are to go. Since we have not
passed this way before, it is important to look unto
Jesus, the Author and Finisher of our faith.

Not only were the Israelites told to go after the
ark and to keep their distance from it but they were
told to "sanctify themselves" (v. 5). And that is in
keeping with what we have been considering. No
activity requires sanctification more than occupation
with the Lord Jesus. It is written, "Be ye holy; for
I am holy" (I Peter 1:16).

If we do this, *His way* will be clear to us, and
His wonders will be performed among us. The mere
desire to see His wonders is not enough. There are
certain prerequisites, but they are not impossible to
come by. If we set our minds on things above where
Christ sitteth at the right hand of God, we shall find
that the rest will follow in due course. The promise
to Israel was, "Tomorrow the LORD will do wonders
among you." The driving back of the Jordan, and
their actual entry into the land, were included in
that promise. The spiritual import of this we shall
see later.

Before we proceed, we are permitted to hear a
further word to Joshua himself. It was the first word
addressed to him directly since that word of en-

couragement recorded in Joshua 1:9. He who had been making much of the ark, which typified Christ, was now told that he also was going to be magnified in the sight of all Israel (v. 7), and then the Lord repeated the promise that as He was with Moses so He would be with him.

This interruption, if it may be called that, is very interesting. From it we may learn that those who honor their Lord shall, in turn, be honored by Him. To all such the Lord pledges, as it were, His continued fellowship, saying, "I will be with thee." To be honored by the Lord is wonderful! But to be honored by His personal presence is even more wonderful! Such was the honor bestowed upon Joshua. And it is still true that "them that honor me I will honor" (I Sam. 2:30).

THE ROAD TO GREATNESS

Apart from the commands which Joshua gave, there was nothing outstanding about what he did here. He seems to have been in the background most of the time. We do not read that he was one of those who carried the ark, nor do we read that he accompanied it into the raging waters of the Jordan. There was nothing spectacular about anything that he did. But all the while the Lord was magnifying him in the sight of all Israel. Such was the behavior of one who was truly great. How prone most of us are to push ourselves forward in order to be noticed, forgetting that it is true greatness to serve unseen and to work unnoticed.

The authority of Joshua appears to have been complete. Not only were the people under his direct command but the priests also took their orders from him. It was he who instructed them to take up the ark and to go over before the people, and they obeyed him (v. 6).

At this point Joshua received fresh instructions from the Lord, who reassured him that as He was with Moses so He would be with him. He was told to "command the priests that bear the ark of the covenant, saying, When ye are come to the brink of the water of Jordan, ye shall stand still in Jordan." Perhaps they had been wondering what they were to do next. But a step at a time seems to be God's way for those who walk the path of faith. With full confidence in Him who knows the end from the beginning, it is not necessary for us to see very far ahead, "for we walk by faith, and not by sight" (II Cor. 5:7).

To men of the world this may look like a hazardous way of doing things. But even they recognize that a leader is often called upon to take risks. Barnabas and Paul were described as men that had "hazarded their lives for the name of our Lord Jesus Christ" (Acts 15:26). And Paul could say of Epaphroditus that "for the work of Christ he was nigh unto death, not regarding his life" (Phil. 2:30). The R.S.V. renders this "risking his life." Such is the mark of true disciples of the Lord Jesus. "Who follows in their train?"

We read, in verse 9 of this chapter, that Joshua resumed his instructions to the people as a whole. His first command to them had been "Prepare you victuals" (Joshua 1:11). The second command may be summed up in the words, "Hallow [or, sanctify] yourselves" (3:5). His third command sounds more like an invitation: "Come hither, and hear the words of the LORD your God" (v. 9).

That which follows leaves us in no doubt about the spiritual significance of the ark. It was by the ark that the Israelites were to know, first of all, that the living God was among them. Second, they were to know that He would without fail drive out from before them the seven nations then in possession of the land. Thus they were assured of the divine presence in their midst and of the divine power working in their behalf.

What more could they ask? "Behold, the ark of the covenant of the Lord of all the earth passeth over before you into Jordan" (v. 11). They had never heard the ark spoken of in that way before. Previous to this it was simply referred to as the ark of the covenant. But now it is to be known as the ark of the covenant of the Lord of all the earth. The God of Israel is no mere "tribal deity." Even Rahab had acknowledged, "He is God in heaven above, and in the earth beneath" (Joshua 2:11). That ark was the symbol by which He vouchsafed His personal presence and power.

THE CERTAINTY OF FAITH

Immediately after this the Israelites were instructed to select twelve men, one out of each tribe, of whom we shall hear more in the next chapter. The priests who bore the ark were all taken from the tribe of Levi, but here we see a group of men who were to be representatives of the whole nation.

We are not told, as yet, why they were chosen. It does not appear that they themselves inquired about that, all of which manifests fullest confidence in the Lord and His servant.

But Joshua did not leave the people in doubt as to what was about to happen. "It shall come to pass," said he, "as soon as the soles of the feet of the priests that bear the ark of the LORD, the Lord of all the earth, shall rest in the waters of Jordan, that the waters of Jordan shall be cut off from the waters that come down from above; and they shall stand upon an heap" (v. 13). There was no guesswork about this. He did not say, "Now if we do thus and so, so and so ought to happen." He predicted exactly what would take place.

Of course, there are those who would explain this on purely natural grounds. It is presumed that there was an earthquake upstream that temporarily dammed up the river. Well, suppose such was the case. Even if the Lord did use such means to accomplish this miracle, the revelation of it to Joshua, and the perfect timing of it, compel us to believe that what took place was due to supernatural power.

The east wind has blown over the Red Sea many times since the Exodus, but we have not heard of any repetition of the miracle that took place at that time. The same One who caused and timed the earthquakes that took place when our Lord arose from the dead and when Paul and Silas were in the prison at Philippi, might have used similar means to cut off the waters of the Jordan. But when the question is raised in Psalm 114 as to what ailed the Jordan that it was "turned back," it is made quite clear that "the presence of the God of Jacob" caused the earth to tremble (cf. Psalm 114:7). The living God was present at the Jordan, and the ark of the covenant was the visible symbol of His presence.

Jordan was at its worst when all this took place. It was overflowing all of its banks. But it was harvest time. Close by were fields of ripened grain ready for the reaper. Almost forty years had rolled by since the spies first brought back samples of the fruits of this land flowing with milk and honey. Now the people could see for themselves what their fathers had missed because of their unbelief at Kadesh. Let us beware lest we also be "fools, and slow of heart to believe all" that the Lord has spoken concerning our heavenly inheritance.

The spiritual significance of the concurrence of

the overflowing of the Jordan with the time of harvest becomes quite clear when considered as an illustration of what our Lord endured at Calvary in order that He might see the fruit of the travail of His soul and be satisfied. In Psalm 69 we hear Him say prophetically, "The waters are come in unto my soul . . . . I am come into deep waters, where the floods overflow me." And again, "Let not the waterflood overflow me, neither let the deep swallow me up."

Such was His experience when He became obedient unto death *"even* the death of the cross" (Phil. 2:8). The measure of the unspeakable horrors of such a death is indicated in the words, "My God, my God, why hast thou forsaken me?" But for the sake of the harvest, and for the joy that was set before Him, He endured the cross and despised the shame, "and is set down at the right hand of the throne of God" (Heb. 12:2).

In Joshua 3:16 we are told that "the waters which came down from above stood and rose up upon an heap very far from the city Adam, that is beside Zaretan." This reference to Adam is both interesting and instructive. It was through Adam that sin and death entered this world. "By one man sin entered into the world, and death by sin" (Rom. 5:12). But it was through death that our blessed Lord rendered powerless him who had the might of death, that is, the devil, that He might "deliver them who through fear of death were all their lifetime subject to bondage" (Heb. 2:14-15).

When He suffered for sin and all of its dread consequences, He went right back to the root of it all—back to the sin of Adam himself. Thus God showed forth "his righteousness for the remission of sins that are past, through the forbearance of God; to declare, . . . at this time his righteousness: that he might be just, and the justifier of him which believeth in Jesus" (Rom. 3:25-26).

When God forgave the sins of Old Testament believers He did so in view of the cross. The blood of bulls and goats could never take away sins (Heb. 10:4). The sacrifices offered in Old Testament times may be likened to our paper money. They were "legal tender" for the time being, but they all pointed to the one perfect Sacrifice. When He came, He fulfilled all those types, gave form to all the figures, and substance to all the shadows of the law (cf. Heb. 9:25; 10:1).

The closing verses of our chapter show that the Jordan was not only turned back but it was also cut off. Those waters that came down toward the sea of the plain, that is the Dead Sea, failed, and were cut off, "and *all* the Israelites passed over on dry ground, until *all* the people were passed clean over Jordan." Not one soul was left behind. All of the Lord's people shared in this wonderful victory over that which stands for death and all its terrors.

"And the priests that bare the ark of the covenant stood firm on dry ground in the midst of Jordan" till the very last one had crossed. They were faithful and fearless till their work was done. We believe that there is a lesson in all of this for us. Their first duty was to "take up the ark" (v. 6). Next, they were to "pass over before the people." Then they were to "stand still in Jordan" (v. 8). When we take into consideration the number of people who had to cross, we may get some idea of the amount of patience and courage which this last required.

For the priests to stand in a place of impending danger, where the waters might descend upon them at any moment, could not have been very easy. But these priests were equal to it. No doubt it was the ark, and what it stood for, that enabled them to stand there without flinching. On the other hand, we must not belittle their courage. They were undoubtedly courageous men. For that we give them ungrudging credit.

Those priests standing there in Jordan remind us of the words of Milton, "They also serve who only stand and wait." They were serving the Lord's people most effectively even though they were standing still. They were "stedfast, unmoveable" and yet "abounding in the work of the Lord." Their holding up the ark is an example to us who seek to hold up Christ for others to see in order that they may have free access to the blessings which are theirs in Christ. It is a service well worth coveting, and we trust that some who read these lines may be encouraged by this to seek grace from God to render such service.

CHAPTER FIVE

What Mean These Stones?

(Joshua 4)

IN CHAPTER 3 attention is focused on the ark of the covenant. In chapter 4 attention is directed, for the most part, to two groups of stones, twelve in each group. Nothing was said about those stones till all the people had passed over Jordan. Then the twelve men who had been chosen beforehand were directed to take up twelve stones "out of the midst of Jordan, out of the place where the priests' feet stood firm." Those twelve men were representative (vv. 4-5), and so were the stones. That being so, the transfer of those stones to Gilgal must be significant.

Previous to their being transferred, they lay in the place of death, buried beneath the waters of the Jordan, and may well represent those who are dead in trespasses and in sins. The bringing of the ark into the Jordan led to their discovery when the river was driven back "at the presence of the God of Jacob" (Psalm 114). Then the light from heaven shone upon them, revealing their exact location and condition. The ark, which was a type of Him who is the light of the world, had come into the very place where they lay not only that they might be exposed, but that they might be lifted out of the riverbed and set up in Gilgal, the place of deliverance. This is a striking preview of "the grace of God that *bringeth* salvation" (Titus 2:11).

The fact that the stones were taken from the place where the priests' feet stood firm is also suggestive. Those priests standing there, holding up the ark, point to Him at whose feet many precious souls have found deliverance. It was at Jesus' feet that the sinful woman of Luke 7 received the pardon of her sins. It was at Jesus' feet that Mary heard His word, and there she later found heartfelt sympathy in a time of sorrow and bereavement. It is before those same feet that the redeemed will yet cast their crowns as they give their Redeemer their homage and praise.

As set up in Gilgal, those twelve stones were to have a voice for the generations to come. They were intended to provoke the question, "What mean ye by these stones?" (v. 6). That question has two answers. First, those stones meant "that the waters of Jordan were cut off before the ark of the covenant of the LORD; when it passed over [or, went through] Jordan, the waters of Jordan were cut off: and these stones shall be for a memorial unto the children of Israel for ever" (v. 7). Thus those stones became a memorial of a miracle here attributed to the presence of the ark.

The ark was inseparably linked with the presence of the Lord. Its cover was known as the mercy seat, where He sat between the cherubims that over-shadowed it (Ps. 80:1). When the ark went forward Moses said, "Rise up, LORD, and let thine enemies be scattered; and let them that hate thee flee before thee. And when it rested, he said, Return, O LORD, unto the many thousands of Israel" (Num. 10:35-36). By means of those stones set up in Gilgal, the coming generations were to know what "the presence of the God of Jacob" (Psalm 114:7) could effect, and that when He undertakes for His people, there is nothing that can withstand His glorious presence. Would that *we* realized these truths more than we do.

The second answer to this question is equally important and interesting. Joshua spoke to the children of Israel saying, "When your children shall ask their fathers in time to come, saying, What mean these stones? then ye shall let your children know, saying, Israel came over this Jordan on dry land. For Jehovah your God dried up the waters of Jordan *before you,* until ye were passed over" (Josuha 4:21-23, A.S.V.).

In verse 7 we see how the waters were *cut off* before the ark. In verse 23 we learn that they were *dried up* from before the people. Thus the Lord graciously gave His people the honor of sharing in the working of this great miracle. Thus did He "divide the spoil with the strong" (Isa. 53:12). The River Jordan, which is a type of "the king of terrors" (Job 18:14), is made to respect His people as they move along under His direction "terrible as an army with banners" (Song of Sol. 6:10).

Finally, the whole thing is compared with what the Lord had done for the older generation at the Red Sea. As a member of that older generation, Joshua could say, "As the LORD your God did to the Red Sea, which He dried up from *before us,* until we were gone over" (v. 23). Truly the lovingkindness of Jehovah "is from everlasting to everlasting upon them that fear him, and his righteousness unto children's children; to such as keep his covenant and to those that remember his precepts to do them" (cf. Ps. 103:17-18, A.S.V.). From generation to generation He is the same. We change; He changes not. Great is His faithfulness!

But this memorial was to serve a still wider purpose. It was put there also "that all the people of the earth might know the hand of the LORD, that it is mighty: that ye might fear the LORD your God for ever" (v. 24). What was done there was not to be kept secret. It was to be universally known. In this way the Lord would use His redeemed people to teach the world lessons which it cannot and will not learn in any other way. Yes, even the principalities and powers in the heavenlies will have the manifold wisdom of God made known unto them by the Church (Eph. 3:10), just as the peoples of the earth were to know, through Israel, the might of the Lord.

This memorial was also to have its due effect upon the Israelites, that they might fear the Lord forever. They must not allow the fact that they were so intimately involved in all of this to lessen their reverence for Him and His things. Rather, they were to fear Him forever. So should it ever be with those who profess to know the Lord and His ways. Those who know Him best revere Him most. The remembrance of what He has done for us should make us fear Him and love Him more every day.

TWELVE OTHER STONES

Now let us go back a little and take a look at the other group of twelve stones mentioned in verse 9 of Joshua 4. Their number indicates that they, like the first twelve, are also representative. They were set in exactly the same place, "where the feet of the priests which bare the ark of the covenant stood." But it was Joshua—and Joshua alone—who handled these stones.

In the case of the first group, it was the twelve men who took up, every man of them, a stone upon his shoulder, "according unto the number of the tribes of the children of Israel" (v. 5). That was their part in the significant transfer from the bed of the Jordan to Gilgal. As such, we may consider these men as typical of ministers of the Lord who serve His people by bearing them upon their hearts as well as on their shoulders in order that they may enjoy the blessings of which Gilgal speaks.

In the case of the second group, the procedure was quite different. As we have remarked, Joshua handled these himself. Instead of being set up in Gilgal, these were "set up . . . in the midst of Jordan" (v. 9). And even though they were not removed from the riverbed they were separated from the other stones there. Henceforth they are no longer typical of those who are dead *in* trespasses and *in* sins, but of those who are dead *to* sin. When the waters of Jordan returned and covered them they were no longer like those who are swallowed up in their sins, but rather like those who have been buried with Christ (cf. Rom. 6:4). "Old things are passed away; behold, all things are become new" (II Cor. 5:17).

That the Jordan may teach different lessons at the same time presents no difficulty if we remember that the Red Sea meant one thing to the Israelites; quite another to the Egyptians (cf. Heb. 11:29).

From Romans 6 we learn that we have died to sin and that we are buried with Christ by baptism unto death. We have become identified with Him in the likeness of His death. Our old man has been crucified with Him in order that the body of sin, that is, sin in its totality, might be annulled, so that we should no longer serve sin. And if we have become identified with Him in the likeness of His death, "we shall be also in the likeness of his resurrection" (Rom. 6:5).

The two groups of stones which we have been considering serve, we believe, as illustrations of faith reckoning these truths of our having died with Christ (Col. 2:20) and having been raised with Him (3:1) to be facts. Stones, being completely passive, illustrate the truth that all is done *for* the believer not *by* him. "Likewise reckon ye also yourselves to be dead indeed unto sin, but alive unto God through Jesus Christ our Lord" (Rom. 6:11).

TRANSFORMED

Those twelve stones which were taken up out of Jordan, which Joshua set up in Gilgal, may now be looked upon as "living stones" (I Peter 2:5). We do not usually think of stones as being alive, hence the familiar expression, "dead as a stone." And yet when one holds a precious stone under a light so that it may sparkle in all of its beauty, people will exclaim, "It fairly lives!" And so it does. But what makes it live? The light that shines upon it and through it. That may help us to understand how it is that we may be spoken of as "living stones." While in our sins we lay in nature's darkness. But God has called us out of darkness into His marvelous light, that we may show forth His virtues (Cf. I Peter 2:9).

But not every stone sparkles. A diamond is a stone, but not every stone is a diamond. And yet the brilliant diamond is but carbon transformed in God's own laboratory, so that it may show forth the glories of the light that shines upon it.

Just how this transformation is effected may be illustrated by another group of twelve stones, which also represented God's people. I refer to the twelve stones which Elijah used to build an altar in those dark days when the nation of Israel had turned from the living God to worship Baal. There was so little light and life left in Israel that Elijah thought he was the only faithful one remaining. But when he repaired the altar of the Lord which was broken down, he "took twelve stones, according to the number of the tribes of the sons of Jacob, unto whom the word of the LORD came, saying, Israel shall be

thy name: and with the stones he built an altar in
the name of the LORD" (I Kings 18:31-32).

In verse 38 of the same chapter we are told that
those stones were consumed by the fire of the Lord.
But we may be sure that they were not destroyed.
They represented the sons of Jacob, to whom it was
said, "Thy name shall be called no more Jacob, but
Israel: for as a prince hast thou power with God
and with men, and hast prevailed" (Gen. 32:28).
For God to practically effect that change in Jacob,
he had to be put into the crucible in order that the
fire of the Lord might transform him into a gem
that will forever reflect the glories of the great Re-
finer and Lapidary.

It takes more than one stone, however, to tell
the whole story of redeeming and transforming grace.
Accordingly, we find in the breastplate of Aaron
twelve precious stones "with the names of the children of Israel" engraven upon them. Thus Aaron
bore the names of the children of Israel upon his
heart when he went into the holy place "for a memorial before the LORD continually" (Exodus 28:
29). "The rainbow of the spray" may give us a
fleeting view of God's manifold grace, but those
twelve stones are like the stars that shine forever and
ever.

EVERYONE REPRESENTED

Returning now to Joshua 4, we find all of this
connected with the fact that "the children of Reuben,
and the children of Gad, and half the tribe of
Manasseh, passed over before the children of Israel,
as Moses spake unto them: about forty thousand
prepared for war passed over before the LORD unto
battle, to the plains of Jericho" (vv. 12-13).

In addition to what we have already learned about
that monument in Gilgal, we also learn that it de-

picted the unity of God's people. Even the two and one-half tribes were represented in this monument. Though they had claimed their possessions east of the Jordan, they were one with their brethren who had not yet entered into their inheritance. A practical demonstration of that unity is seen in the action of the forty thousand who passed over armed before the Lord to join with their brethren in the conquest of their inheritance. We may talk about unity, but unless we are prepared to stand shoulder to shoulder with our brethren in Christ against a common foe, there will be no practical results.

It is in immediate connection with this that the Scripture says, "On that day the LORD magnified Joshua in the sight of all Israel" (v. 14). It was a great day. And God used the occasion to honor His faithful servant Joshua. With the lessons of those two monuments fresh in their minds the Israelites could properly appreciate the one whom the Lord had raised up to succeed Moses. "And they feared him, as they feared Moses, all the days of his life."

Then, fully confirmed as their divinely-chosen leader, Joshua was told to command the priests who bore the ark of the testimony to come up out of Jordan. As soon as they did, "the waters of Jordan returned unto their place, and flowed over all his banks, as they did before" (v. 18).

From this we may learn that what the Lord does for His own abides and is effective until all of His redeemed ones have "passed clean over." There is something very precious and also very solemn about that. It is precious because it assures us that not one of His own shall fail to cross over into the land which God had promised them. On the other hand, it is solemn because He made no provision for retreat. To have left that way open would have invited

retreat. But He did not do that. Likewise God's
children today are not to be "of them who draw
back unto perdition; but of them that believe to
the saving of the soul" (Heb. 10:39).

A SOLEMN REMINDER

"And the people came up out of Jordan on the
tenth day of the first month," which was the very
day on which each household was to take a lamb
in preparation for the Passover (Exodus 12:3). It
was the fortieth anniversary of their deliverance
from the bondage of Egypt. On that occasion the
waters of the Red Sea drowned their enemies, and
at the same time put an impassable barrier between
them and Egypt. On this occasion, as it were, the
return of the Jordan committed them to conflicts
ahead. There was but one way to move, and that
was forward.

The effect of all this upon the people of the land
is seen in the opening verse of Joshua 5, where God
permits us to look behind the scenes. There we see
two groups: "all the kings of the Amorites, which
were on the side of Jordan westward, and all the
kings of the Canaanites, which were by the sea."

It may be that in the former are those which
represent the principalities and powers under the
direct control of the devil; and in the latter, "the
children of disobedience," human beings, in whom
the same spirit now works (Eph. 2:2). But that is
only a suggestion. One thing was true of both groups
of kings: "their heart melted, neither was there
spirit in them any more, because of the children of
Israel." No doubt their utter lack of morale is here
revealed for the encouragement of the Israelites.
Their enemies had been thrown into a panic.

It is important to notice that it was not the nu-
merical strength of the Israelites nor their material

equipment for battle that produced this effect. It was when they heard "that the LORD had dried up the waters of Jordan from before the children of Israel, . . . that their heart melted." It was not what the Israelites were, nor what they had done, that struck terror to the hearts of the Canaanites and the Amorites. It was what the Lord had done. The "east wall" of their kingdom had been pierced by One who was mightier than they. It was the beginning of the end for them.

If we could look behind the scenes, as by faith we may, we would discover a similar state of affairs among the hosts of Satan. An old saying puts it well; "The devil trembles when he sees the weakest saint upon his knees." Scripture tells us to resist the devil, and he will flee from us (James 4:7). But we must resist him steadfastly in the faith (I Peter 5:9). And "the people that do know their God shall be strong, and do exploits" (Dan. 11:32).

CHAPTER SIX

The Last Step Before Victory

(Joshua 5:2-12)

FROM THE HUMAN VIEWPOINT, if ever there was a
time to strike at the Canaanites it was right after the
Israelites had gained entrance to the land. Fear had
taken hold on the inhabitants of Palestine. But divine plans are not made according to human strategy. Before the Lord would give His people complete victory over their enemies He must teach them
another very important lesson. This He did by commanding them to renew the rite of circumcision,
which had been neglected for many years. Since the
generation born in the wilderness had not been circumcised, the renewal of the rite is here referred to
as "the second time" (Joshua 5:2).

Circumcision was the sign of a covenant between
Jehovah and His people (Gen. 17:9-14). According to Romans 4:11, Abraham received circumcision as a seal of the righteousness of the faith he
had. Circumcision involved obedience to the will of
God; disobedience nullified it altogether (cf. Rom.
2:25). A circumcised man was a debtor to do the
whole law. Abraham, however, was not under the
law of Moses, even as we Christians are not under
it. Therefore we need not hesitate to inquire what
meaning this might have for us.

In Colossians 2:11 we are taught that as Christians we have been circumcised with a circumcision

not done by hand and that it signifies the putting
off of the body of the flesh. "In Christ you were
circumcised, not by any physical act, but by being
set free from the sins of the flesh by virtue of Christ's
circumcision" (Phillips). It is "the operation of
God."

The fact that this Christian circumcision is linked
with burial and resurrection (Col. 2:11-12) agrees
perfectly with what we have had before us in our
study of Joshua 4. The twelve stones which Joshua
set up in the midst of Jordan depict our burial with
Christ, whereas the stones set up in Gilgal speak of
resurrection with Him. These are facts which depend
not upon our experience but on the word of God.
And faith takes God at His word. Faith reckons
what God has said about our death and resurrection
with Christ to be so now.

Lest it be thought that we are reading too much
into the passage which we are studying, let us see
what significance there is attached to the renewal
of the rite of circumcision. In that connection we
observe that after everything had been accomplished
Jehovah said to Joshua, "This day have I rolled
away the reproach of Egypt from off you" (v. 9).

WHAT IS THE REPROACH OF EGYPT?

Some think that this expression means "the reproach which proceeds from Egypt." In other words,
it was the reproach with which the Egyptians would
have reproached the Israelites if the Lord had failed
to bring them into the land according to His promise.
In that case, it would signify one of two things:
either that He had cast them aside as unfit to enter
the land, or that He Himself had been frustrated in
attempting to bring them in.

There are a number of Scriptures which apparently support this view. After Israel had broken the

law and the Lord had threatened to consume them, we hear Moses saying, "Wherefore should the Egyptians speak, and say, For mischief did he bring them out, to slay them in the mountains, and to consume them from the face of the earth?" (Exodus 32:12).

Then, at Kadesh-barnea they refused to enter the land and even planned to return to Egypt. Because of this the Lord threatened to smite them with pestilence and to disinherit them. But Moses interceded for them, saying, "Then the Egyptians shall hear it, . . . and they will tell it to the inhabitants of this land: . . . if thou shalt kill all this people as one man, then the nations which have heard the fame of thee will speak, saying, Because the LORD was not able to bring this people into the land which he sware unto them, therefore he hath slain them in the wilderness" (Num. 14:13-16; cf. Deut. 9:28).

Moreover, we heard the Lord Himself saying, "I said, I would scatter them into corners, I would make the remembrance of them to cease from among men: were it not that I feared the wrath of the enemy, lest their adversaries should behave themselves strangely, and lest they should say, Our hand is high, and the LORD hath not done all this" (Deut. 32:26-27). And that certainly would have been a reproach to them and to the Lord.

But if that is what "the reproach of Egypt" means, then it would have required nothing more than their successful entry into Canaan to roll it away. But it was not after their entry into the land, but upon the renewal of the rite of circumcision that the Lord said, "This day have I rolled away the reproach of Egypt from off you."

THE BADGE OF FREEDOM

In view of this, it seems clear that the reproach of Egypt is not the reproach which would have come from Egypt in case they failed to enter the land but, rather, a reproach connected with their uncircumcision.

In connection with this it has been inferred that circumcision was prohibited to the Hebrews while they were slaves in Egypt because it was the distinctive mark of the ruling class. This seems to be confirmed by a passage in the book of Ezekiel (32:19) where the judgment of "the multitude of Egypt" includes their being "laid with the uncircumcised." There would not be much point to that if they themselves were uncircumcised.

In any case, circumcision would not have the same significance for an Egyptian which it had for an Israelite. To him it was a token of his relationship to God. It marked him out as a son of Abraham to whom it was given as a sign and a seal. Lacking it, no Israelite might eat the Passover. In such a case he would have no more right than a stranger or a hired servant (Exodus 12:43-50). And that would be to his reproach. Thus we can see that if the Israelites were prohibited from receiving this mark of distinction while in Egypt that would be, in a very real sense, a reproach.

But there is still another way in which we may consider this matter. Even if the Egyptians did practice circumcision, in God's sight they were no better than the uncircumcised. For example, in Jeremiah 9:25-26 we read, "Behold, the days come, saith the LORD, that I will punish all them which are circumcised with the uncircumcised; Egypt, and Judah, and Edom, and the children of Ammon, and Moab, . . . for all these nations are uncircumcised, and all the house of Israel are uncircumcised in the heart."

What all of this means to us as Christians may be seen in Ephesians 2:11-12, where the Apostle Paul writes, "Wherefore remember, that ye being in time past Gentiles in the flesh, who are called Uncircumcision [plainly, a term of reproach] by that which is called the Circumcision in the flesh made by hands; that at that time ye were without Christ, being aliens from the commonwealth of Israel, and strangers from the covenants of promise, having no hope, and without God in the world."

Such was the spiritual state of the Egyptians in Moses' day. For the people of God to be enslaved to such would be a reproach indeed. Israel's failure to take unto themselves the badge of freedom as soon as they were delivered from the bondage of Egypt is just another illustration of how slow God's people are to avail themselves of their God-given rights and privileges. Even after the Israelites had entered the land of Canaan, it was not until they were commanded to be circumcised that they again received this mark of distinction. But when they did, the Lord said that He had rolled away from them the reproach of Egypt.

We Christians have been circumcised in a spiritual sense with "the circumcision made without hands," and this has been effected in and by the cross of our Lord Jesus Christ. This is wholly a divine operation, and it has most blessed results. We are "no more strangers and foreigners, but fellowcitizens with the saints, and of the household of God" (Eph. 2:19). We have been delivered from the power, or authority, of darkness and have been translated into the kingdom of the Son of God's love (Col. 1:13).

WHAT DIFFERENCE DOES IT MAKE?

All of this should have a very practical effect upon our lives. For a circumcised Israelite to live like an

Egyptian would have been a denial of the very thing his circumcision signified. By it he was to be distinguished and separated from all others. And by it he was committed to keep the law of Moses.

In like manner, our Christian circumcision distinguishes and separates us from the world, and by it we are committed to lovingly obey Him who has set us free from the tyranny of sin and Satan. We are not to walk "as other Gentiles walk, in the vanity of their mind, having the understanding darkened, being alienated from the life of God through the ignorance that is in them, because of the blindness of their heart: who being past feeling have given themselves over to lasciviousness, to work all uncleanness with greediness," for we have not so learned Christ (Eph. 4:17-20).

Immediately after the reproach of Egypt was rolled away from off them, "the children of Israel encamped in Gilgal," which means "a rolling away." There they "kept the passover on the fourteenth day of the month at even in the plains of Jericho." As far as the record goes, this was the third time in the history of the nation that this sacred feast was observed by them.

It was celebrated for the first time in Egypt, of course. Then it was celebrated again at Sinai (Num. 9:5). But we do not read of any other celebration until they came to Gilgal. And there it was accompanied by something most interesting and instructive. "They did eat of the old corn of the land on the morrow after the passover, unleavened cakes, and parched corn in the selfsame day. And the manna ceased on the morrow after they had eaten of the old corn of the land; neither had the children of Israel manna any more; but they did eat of the fruit of the land of Canaan that year" (Joshua 5:11-12).

The wilderness journey was over and with it the wilderness provision ceased. And its cessation was as miraculous as its creation. Like the miraculous gifts and powers which marked the inauguration of the Church, the manna ceased when its purpose was fulfilled. It was a temporary ration, so to speak. For the conflicts before them the children of Israel would require a different kind of food, one which had in it the germ of life. This the manna did not have.

The Lord Jesus said, "Your fathers did eat manna in the wilderness, and are dead" (John 6:49). And again, "Your fathers did eat manna, and are dead" (John 6:58). But then He described Himself as "the bread of God . . . which cometh down from heaven, and giveth life unto the world . . . . This is the bread which cometh down from heaven: that a man may eat thereof and not die" (John 6:33, 50). It is of this bread, we believe, that the old corn of the land speaks. It is a native of "the heavenly places." But it is also the result of death. For "except a corn of wheat fall into the ground and die, it abideth alone: but if it die, it bringeth forth much fruit" (John 12:24).

From this we may learn two very precious things: first, that our blessed Lord gave His life *for* us; second, that He gives His life *to* us. "Christ our passover is sacrificed for us: therefore let us keep the feast, . . . with the unleavened bread of sincerity and truth" (I Cor. 5:7-8).

And so the celebration of a feast closes Israel's preparation for the battle of Jericho. *In a figure,* they had been crucified, buried, and raised again with Christ. And then they fed upon Him. Thus they were divinely prepared for the conflict with the nations of Canaan, types of the wicked spirits in heavenly places.

Ordinary military strategy would have demanded action against the foe long before this. But the plans, as well as the weapons, for this kind of warfare may not be made according to human wisdom. This kind requires divine wisdom, in order that those who go forth to battle may be mighty through God to the pulling down of Satan's strongholds (cf. II Cor. 10:4).

The whole procedure here must have been an enigma to the enemy. Indeed, it must have looked like folly to him. However, our God chooses the foolish things of the world to confound the wise, and the weak things to confound the mighty, in order that no flesh should glory in His presence. But it takes us a long time to learn that lesson.

CHAPTER SEVEN

The Fall of Jericho

(Joshua 5:13—6:27)

BEFORE THE BATTLE of Jericho actually took place, Joshua was granted an extraordinary vision, that of a man with a drawn sword in his hand. This man was none other than the Lord Himself, appearing in a most unusual role. That this is so, is supported by the fact that the narrative continues with the Lord Himself speaking, with no indication that any other person was present.

It is evident that Joshua did not know at first who this Person was. But "Joshua went unto him, and said unto him, Art thou for us, or for our adversaries?" Satan, as we know from Scripture, is not slow to transform himself into an angel of light (cf. II Cor. 11:14) in order to deceive the children of God. Therefore we are told to try the spirits, to see whether or not they be of God (cf. I John 4:1). That is exactly what Joshua did on this occasion.

When he discovered who it was that stood there before him, he "fell on his face to the earth, and did worship, and said unto him, What saith my Lord unto his servant?" Joshua was a captain, but he recognized in this Person his superior officer. So, like every good soldier, he was ready to obey.

But the first command he received had nothing whatever to do with military matters. He was commanded to loose his shoe from off his foot because

70

the ground he was standing on was holy ground. "And Joshua did so."

This act of reverence and obedience on the part of Joshua is full of instruction for us. If we would fight the battles of the Lord we must know "the captain of our salvation" (Heb. 2:10). One of the greatest soldiers of Jesus Christ that this world has ever seen said his chief desire in life was to know Him (Phil. 3:10), and this desire is the secret of his success as a good soldier of Jesus Christ.

The very ground upon which this Captain stood became hallowed ground because of His presence there. The soil of Canaan, utterly defiled by its filthy inhabitants, is made sacred by the presence of the Lord. That in itself is a strong clue to the identity of this wonderful Person. Isaiah was granted a vision of Him in His glory as the royal Priest whose train filled the temple (John 12:41). Daniel also beheld Him as "the Ancient of days" (Dan. 7:9). Ezekiel saw Him as a man upon a throne of sapphire (Ezek. 1:26). John saw Him "in the midst of the seven golden candlesticks" (Rev. 1:13). John also saw Him as the Rider on a white horse and described Him as one who "in righteousness doth judge and make war" (Rev. 19:11). Joshua's vision of Him was not unlike this last.

We have already remarked that this was a most unusual role for Him. To see Him "with his sword drawn in his hand" indicates that He is about to take vengeance on His enemies. It should be observed in the well-known passage which speaks of "the sword of the Spirit" (Eph. 6:17), that this sword is for the purpose of fighting against wicked spirits in the heavenly places.

The fact that we do not wrestle against flesh and blood in such a conflict is sufficient to show that it is not a battle against human beings. It certainly does not refer to the preaching of the gospel, or of ministry to the people of God. Souls are not born again by sword thrusts but by the incorruptible seed of the living Word of God. Saints are nourished by the sincere milk of the Word, and cleansed by the washing of the water of the Word. The sword is reserved for those who have opposed the truth and Him who is the truth; for enemies and apostates. Therefore when we see the Lord with a drawn sword in His hand we may know that He is about to smite in judgment.

We get a good illustration of these distinctions in Psalm 45. In the second verse of that lovely song the Lord is described as the One who is fairer than the children of men; One into whose lips grace is poured. Evidence of that was seen when He was here on earth ministering in the synagogue at Nazareth, where they "all bare him witness, and wondered at the gracious words which proceeded out of his mouth" (Luke 4:22). But when He girds Himself with His sword (Psalm 45:3) the day of grace will have passed.

When He appeared to Joshua as He did, the day of grace for Jericho, a type of this wicked world, had just about passed. In Abraham's day judgment was delayed because the iniquity of the Amorites was not yet full (Gen. 15:16). But now the day of reckoning had come.

THE PLAN OF BATTLE

Joshua was assured of victory before he began to fight. The Lord said unto him, "See, I have given into thine hand Jericho, and the king thereof, and the mighty men of valour" (Joshua 6:2). How this was to be achieved was then set forth. The Israelites were to compass, or surround, the city in silence once a day for six days (vv. 3, 10).

The host of Israel was divided into distinct parts. First of all came the armed men (vv. 7, 9). Next we see a group of seven priests with trumpets of rams' horns. After them came "the ark of the covenant of the LORD" (v. 8) carried by Levites (I Chron. 15: 2). Finally, there was also a rearguard (vv. 9, 13), "after the ark."

Nothing is said about Joshua's part in this procession. Neither is "the captain of the LORD's host" mentioned. But we know that Joshua was there to give commands (vv. 6, 10, 16). We can only imagine the excitement which must have prevailed in the camp of Israel. But we are told that "Joshua rose early in the morning, and the priests took up the ark of the LORD" (v. 12). It is early in the morning that the soldiers of Jesus Christ gain fresh strength for the battles of the day. Many suffer defeat because they do not meet their Captain in the morning. Joshua's example is a good one for us to follow.

Each group in this procession had its own particular part to perform. The armed men in the first division may well represent those who have taken unto themselves the whole armor of God (Eph. 6:13) in order that they may contend with those who are typical of wicked spirits in heavenly places.

In the second division of Joshua's army were the priests with the trumpets. They constituted the audible part of the host while the people remained silent. Their trumpets were actually jubilee trumpets, such as were used to proclaim liberty throughout the land (Lev. 25:9-10). That being so, we like to think that there was still opportunity for any inhabitant of Jericho to be saved if he would but surrender. We recall that when Jonah proclaimed the overthrow of Nineveh, the Ninevites repented and God spared the city.

The blowing of the trumpets at Jericho would

seem to indicate that God was waiting to be gracious. The fact that there just seven priests were delegated to blow the trumpets is interesting. The number suggests perfection and completeness and may even suggest finality. It was Jericho's last opportunity, which, alas, turned out to be its lost opportunity.

There was one home in that doomed city, however, to which the sound of those trumpets came as sweet music. What meant judgment to most, meant deliverance to those living there. Those trumpets proclaimed life and liberty to Rahab and her household. We get a similar thought in II Corinthians 2: 15-16, where we read that "We are unto God a sweet savour of Christ, in them that are saved, and in them that perish: to the one we are the savour of death unto death; and to the other the savour of life unto life."

The most important part of this procession was undoubtedly the ark. Its normal place was in the holiest of all, where the atmosphere was always fragrant because of the sweet incense burning in the censer of the high priest. The garments of the priests, likewise, would be permeated with the same fragrance. All of that links up quite naturally with II Corinthians 2:15-16.

The ark itself was a type of Christ, whom God set forth to be a mercy seat through faith in His blood (Rom. 3:25). The priests who bore the ark needed not to say anything. The ark spoke for itself, as it were. But what a privilege to carry it! That was not granted to all.

But there was a division in the procession called "the rereward," or rear guard, which apparently consisted of "the people." All could not occupy a place of prominence, but all who took part in this procession were identified with the ark and all that it stood for. Its importance is indicated by the number of times it is mentioned in this chapter. Earlier it is significantly called "the ark of the LORD, the Lord of all the earth" (Joshua 3:11, 13).

GOD'S WAYS ARE STRANGE

No doubt all of this must have looked very foolish to the men of Jericho. What a strange way to go about taking a city! But God says, "My thoughts are not your thoughts, neither are your ways my ways" (Isa. 55:8).

Evidently none of the Israelites questioned this procedure. That, it seems to me, is beautiful evidence of their confidence in the Lord. They were doing His work in His way. Except for the sound of the trumpets, not a voice was to be heard as they marched around Jericho. But that orderly march must have been eloquent in its silence. Like Paul, Joshua must have rejoiced as he beheld their order and the steadfastness of their faith (cf. Col. 2:5).

Somewhere in that week there must have been a sabbath. Perhaps the very last day was a sabbath. The expression "the seventh day" may suggest that (Joshua 6:15). If so, it is all the more wonderful that instead of a halt being called in the proceedings, we find more intense effort being put forth, because on that day they went around the city seven times. Thus the God of all grace was giving ample opportunity for any to repent before He poured out His wrath upon that wicked city.

It was not until the last long blast was sounded by the trumpeters that Joshua gave the commandment to shout. "And the people shouted with a great shout," and the wall fell down flat (v. 20). Some would attribute this to an earthquake, or to the mining of the walls by the Israelites. But neither

is hinted at in the text. The time is coming when
He whose voice — uttered through His people —
shook the walls of Jericho will shake both heaven
and earth (Heb. 12:26). The fact that the walls of
that city did fall as stated has been confirmed by
archaeologists. And the Scripture says, "By faith the
walls of Jericho fell down, after they were com-
passed about seven days" (Heb. 11:30).

And "by faith the harlot Rahab perished not
with *them that believed not*" (Heb. 11:31). For
her and her household, that day was a day of salvation. The word had gone forth, "Rahab the harlot
shall live, she and all that are with her in the house,
because she hid the messengers that we sent"
(Joshua 6:17). In the flush of victory Joshua did
not forget Rahab and her family. He was speaking
for the God of all grace, the same One who had
saved Noah and his family.

There was a difference, however. Noah and his
family were saved by means of an ark. But Rahab
remained in her house, built on the very walls which
fell down flat. Only God could discriminate in this
way. When His judgment strikes in a day yet to
come, "then shall two be in the field; the one shall
be taken, and the other left. Two women shall be
grinding at the mill; the one shall be taken, and
the other left" (Matt. 24:40-41). "The Lord knoweth them that are his" (II Tim. 2:19).

Rahab was saved because she received the Lord's
messengers. In receiving them, she received Him,
for, as He said later, "He that receiveth you receiveth me, and he that receiveth me receiveth him
that sent me" (Matt. 10:40). That seems to be the
reason why such emphasis is put on her reception
of the messengers more than on anything else that
she did. It was true even then that "as many as received him, to them gave he power to become the

sons of God, even to them that believe on his name" (John 1:12).

Rahab was not only saved but she was also given a place to dwell among the Israelites. If she is the same Rahab that is mentioned in Matthew 1:5— and there is reason to believe that she is—then we see that she was not only tolerated among the Israelites but she actually came into the royal line and ancestry of David, and thus of our blessed Lord.

Truly, that was "grace upon grace." Such is the grace of God that takes the beggar from the dunghill that He may set him among princes and make him to inherit the throne of glory (I Sam. 2:8). Nothing short of such royal association is in His plan and purpose for all those who put their trust in Him.

What gratitude must have filled the hearts of Rahab and her family when they saw what they had been saved *from!* But how much more wonderful to see what they had been saved *for!* We can only wonder how many more might have shared in this blessing had they, like Rahab, believed the message of the spies.

RISK BRINGS REWARD

At least one more thing should be noticed here in connection with Rahab and her loved ones. The spies whom she received were the very ones who were sent to bring her out with all that she had (Joshua 6:22). The ones who had risked their lives (cf. Acts 15:25-26) when they went into Jericho with the messsage that saved Rahab and her house, are now sent back to reap the reward of their labor. This may serve as an illustration of I Thessalonians 2:19-20 where the apostle asks, "What is our hope, or joy, or crown of rejoicing? Are not even ye in the presence of our Lord Jesus Christ at his com-

ing? For ye are our glory and joy." The reward in
that day will not consist of some material crown.
The real crown of rejoicing for God's servants will
be the precious souls whom the Lord has been
pleased to save through their labors here.

One likes to think that the loved ones of the
spies—their wives perhaps—who followed them with
their prayers as they undertook the hazardous task
would share in the reward with them. In a similar
connection David said, "As his part is that goeth
down to the battle, so shall his part be that tarrieth
by the stuff: they shall part alike" (I Sam. 30:24).

It is not given to all of us to do that which is
dangerous and spectacular. But we may hold up the
hands of such in prayer. God alone knows the
anxiety that often fills the heart of a beloved helpmeet while her husband is on some dangerous mission for his Lord. But we are persuaded that such
will receive their due reward at the judgment seat
of Christ.

After Rahab and her family had been brought out
of Jericho, the city was burned "with fire, and all
that was therein: only the silver, and the gold, and
the vessels of brass and iron, they put into the
treasury of the house of the LORD" (v. 24). Only that
which could be tried by fire was saved; all the rest
was destroyed.

Then Joshua adjured them at that time, saying,
"Cursed be the man before the LORD, that riseth up
and buildeth this city Jericho: he shall lay the
foundation thereof in his firstborn and in his young-
est son shall be set up the gates of it" (v. 26).

In spite of this, we know from the later history
of Israel that there was a man who attempted it
and suffered accordingly. In the days of the wicked
King Ahab, "Hiel the Bethe-lite" rebuilt Jericho,
but at a cost—the lives of both his eldest and young-

est sons, exactly as it was foretold here. Such is the awful cost of defying the word of the living God. In so doing, Hiel put himself in a class with Cain, the first city-builder, and with the men of Babel, who apparently tried to perpetuate the Cainite civilization after the flood by building a city and a tower whose top would reach to heaven.

The confusion of tongues, which is still with us, is the solemn evidence of God's judgment on that enterprise. The destruction of Sodom and Gomorrah continued the sad tale. The overthrow of Jericho was further evidence of God's determination to wipe out these centers of wickedness and defiance of the living God. Still later, Nineveh and Babylon suffered a similar fate. No doubt these things are intended to teach us that all that man has built up in defiance of God is doomed to destruction.

Thank God, we—like Abram, who was a witness of the destruction of Sodom and Gomorrah—look for a city which hath foundations, whose Architect and Builder is God. Its foundations are laid in the mountains of His holiness (Ps. 87). That will be the true Eternal City. It cost the "firstborn among many brethren" His life, but it shall stand forever. Its gates shall never close, and all the kings of the earth shall bring their glory into it. "And the name of the city from that day shall be, The LORD is there" (Ezek. 48:35).

And so the first grand division of the book of Joshua closes with the note that "the LORD was with Joshua; and his fame was noised throughout all the country" (v. 27). The Lord was with him. That was Joshua's best reward, the presence of the Lord Himself. What more could he ask? Our Lord Jesus said, "Where I am, there shall also my servant be" (John 12:26).

CHAPTER EIGHT

The Battle of Ai

(Joshua 7 and 8)

THE OPENING OF THIS CHAPTER presents a sad contrast to the close of the previous chapter. There we read that "the LORD was with Joshua; and his fame was noised throughout all the country." Here we read, "But the children of Israel committed a trespass [or, unfaithfulness] in the accursed thing."

Thus we see how a great victory may be followed by shameful defeat. It seems to be a rather common experience that we are never in greater danger than right after we have won a great victory. Our adversary, the devil, is quick to take advantage of such an occasion.

In connection with that we recall that Abram, returning from the slaughter of the kings (Gen. 14: 1-16), was approached by the king of Sodom with an offer which, if accepted, might have ruined the wonderful testimony of that man of faith. It was well for him that before the offer was actually made, Melchizedek, "the priest of the most high God" (Heb. 7:1), intercepted him with "bread and wine" (Gen. 14:17).

It was this ministry that strengthened Abram so that he was able to refuse to take anything from the king of Sodom "from a thread even to a shoe-latchet." And thus he won a victory even more important than the one he had just gained on the battlefield. One likes to think that we have here more than a suggestion of a similar ministry from the hands of our blessed High Priest, which, if rightly received, may serve to strengthen us also in our conflict with our foes, seen and unseen. I refer, of course, to the Lord's Supper.

"Fleshly lusts which war against the soul" steal upon us before we are aware of them. Achan coveted the accursed thing, as well as the things that were to go into the treasury of the Lord. And while it is true that in his case there was no Melchizedek to step in between him and the tempter, nevertheless, he did have the warning of Joshua (6:18) to prevent and preserve him.

So far as we know, Achan and his family were the only ones who openly ignored that warning. But the first verse of chapter 7 speaks as though the whole nation was guilty of this sin, unless we take the expression, "the children of Israel" in a restricted sense. But from verses 11 and 12 we gather that the whole nation was involved. There are sins which may be committed in the heart, and covetousness is one of them (cf. Matthew 5:28). Doubtless there were others besides Achan who *saw* and *coveted,* but they did not *take*. Achan confessed all three of these acts.

The fact that Achan was of the royal tribe of Judah would add to the enormity of his sin. Not only did he disobey the command to keep himself from the accursed thing (6:18), but he did so in a time of crisis. The severity of the punishment inflicted upon him is in keeping with these things. And this should be a warning to us who have been blessed with all spiritual blessings in Christ. We have no need to covet the things of this world.

Some may wonder why the enemy should single out a man like Achan to do a thing like this. We gather from verse 1 that he was a man of some importance because his genealogy is given in such detail. To bring a man like that to spiritual ruin would be a victory indeed for the enemy. (Of such strategy we could cite a number of sad examples in our own day and time.) Then, too, there may have been some thought of revenge on the part of our "adversary the devil" because Rahab, saved as a "brand from the burning," had been received into the tribe of Judah.

Again, this may have been a part of Satan's plot to destroy the woman's Seed. The devil was wise enough to know that the line of Abel, reestablished in Seth, was destined to continue through the tribe of Judah. The prophecy of Jacob (Gen. 49: 8-12) makes that clear. Therefore it is not unlikely that Satan was here making another attempt to destroy the Messianic line, and thus, if possible, frustrate the purpose of God who had predicted his defeat through the woman's Seed. The Scripture records a number of such attempts on the part of Pharaoh, Athaliah, Haman, Herod, and others.

THE ENEMY FROM WITHIN

Joshua, unaware of what had taken place in the camp, sent men from Jericho to Ai "to view the country," when there really was more need to look into matters at home. From the report and the recommendation brought back to Joshua (7:3), we gather that there was a good deal of self-confidence, which in this case was just another form of pride. And there is nothing more blinding than pride. While fear, like a magnifying glass, makes the enemy appear greater than he really is, pride makes him appear smaller than he is.

When it suits the enemy's purpose, he makes us afraid. Then, like the spies at Kadesh-barnea, we see him as a formidable giant in whose eyes we look like grasshoppers. But in this case he made himself look like a grasshopper in order to destroy, if possible, through overconfidence, those whom he would not be able to destroy otherwise.

When the Israelites marched around Jericho with the ark of God in their midst, that stronghold fell. But here we read nothing about the ark nor of the well-ordered divisions of the hosts of Israel. Instead, "there went up thither of the people about three thousand men: and they fled before the men of Ai. And the men of Ai smote of them about thirty and six men: for they chased them from before the gate even to Shebarim, and smote them in the going down: wherefore the hearts of the people melted, and became as water" (vv. 4-5).

This temporary success on the part of the enemy may also have filled him with self-confidence. Of course, he was not aware of the fact that he was actually working out the purpose of God, who, through him, was dealing with His own for their ultimate blessing.

Satan may desire to have us that he may sift us, but only to sift us "as wheat" (Luke 22:31). In this way the Lord may use even Satan to get rid of worthless chaff. He may even use him for the destruction of the flesh in order that the spirit may be saved in the day of the Lord Jesus (I Cor. 5:5).

The defeat of Israel brought Joshua and the elders of Israel low before the Lord (v. 6). However, they did not come to confess any failure on their part but rather to inquire of Him why He had allowed all this to happen. They actually blamed Him for having delivered them into the hands of the Amorites to destroy them. It is truly humbling to see in this a picture of our hearts. How often we blame the Lord for some defeat in our lives when we should be asking Him to show us the cause of it that we might confess our part in it.

The answer of the Lord was sharp and abrupt. "Get thee up; wherefore liest thou thus upon thy face? Israel hath sinned" (vv. 10-11). Then He pointed out the cause of their defeat without naming the actual offender. The processes of divine government and discipline must take their due course. The ways of God are deliberate. He is slow to anger. Judgment is His "strange work" (Isa. 28:21).

He might have dealt with Achan directly. But He chose to work through His people. Israel had sinned and they would not be able to stand before their enemies until the accursed thing was removed from among them. The Lord said, "Neither will I be with you any more, except ye destroy the accursed thing from among you" (v. 12). To suffer defeat was bad. To be deprived of His presence was worse.

DEFEAT REVEALS THE SIN

Detailed instructions were given to guide them in their discovery of the one who was directly responsible for all of this trouble, and in dealing with him. In view of all this, we wonder how one who knew that he was guilty, and who must have known that sooner or later he would be discovered, could refrain from making an open confession forthwith. But it was not until he "was taken" that he actually confessed, and then only after Joshua himself urged him to do so.

There seems to be no evidence of real repentance on Achan's part, nor of any sorrow for what he had done, even though he did say, "I have sinned." Judas Iscariot also said, "I have sinned"; but we know from the context that it was not the expression of a truly penitent heart. Nevertheless Achan, as we have already noticed, did admit three things: "I saw . . . I coveted . . . and took" (v. 21).

He saw "among the spoils a goodly Babylonish garment, and two hundred shekels of silver, and a wedge of gold of fifty shekels weight." If, as some believe, the beautiful mantle was woven of golden thread, then all that he took rightly belonged in the treasury of the Lord. In taking these things he was robbing God. Accordingly, it is said in verse 1 of our chapter, "The people of Israel broke faith in regard to the devoted things" (R.S.V.).

The Lord could have exposed Achan in a moment, in the very act of taking these things. But He chose to allow the defeat at Ai to accomplish that, thus involving the whole nation. This leads us to believe that others had coveted the same in their hearts. How true it is that "as in water face answereth to face, so the heart of man to man" (Prov. 27:19). The fact that the record contains not one note of protest when Achan was judged and found guilty would indicate that the judgment was generally approved. And nothing is written about "extenuating circumstances."

The fact that Achan's sons and daughters were condemned with him implies that they were involved. Everything that he owned was involved, even the tent that he lived in (v. 24). "And all Israel stoned him with stones, and burned them with fire, after they had stoned them" (v. 25). With a play on the meaning of Achan's name, Joshua said, "Why has thou *troubled* us? the LORD shall *trouble* thee this day" (v. 25). Achan means "the troubler."

The sadness of this chapter is not altogether unrelieved. It has its bright side also. The place where this solemn event took place was called "the valley of Achor." In the prophecy of Hosea (2:14-15) we read that the day is coming when Jehovah will

allure Israel "and bring her into the wilderness, and
speak comfortably unto her. And I will give her her
vineyards from thence, and *the valley of Achor* for
a door of hope: and she shall sing there, as in the
days of her youth, as in the days when she came
up out of the land of Egypt."

From this it would seem that the chapter we are
studying is in a sense prophetic. According to Jeremiah 30 the nation of Israel will yet go through a
time of unparalleled sorrow, there referred as "the
time of Jacob's trouble, but he shall be saved out
of it" (v. 7). That time of trouble will be to them
a door of hope. The very thought of it makes one
feel like exclaiming with Paul, "O the depth of the
riches both of the wisdom and knowledge of God!
how unsearchable are his judgments, and his ways
past finding out" (Rom. 11:33).

FRESH ENCOURAGEMENT

In keeping with this we find that the next word
from the Lord to Joshua is one of encouragement:
"Fear not, neither be dismayed" (8:1). Similarly,
in the New Testament, right after the Lord Jesus
had spoken of the treason of Judas Iscariot and of
the denial of Peter, He said, "Let not your heart
be troubled."

Here the word of comfort is followed by exact
instructions for the battle of Ai. "Take all the people of war with thee, and arise, go up to Ai: see, I
have given into thy hand the king of Ai, and his
people, and his city, and his land."

Nothing was said about marching around the city.
In fact, the whole plan of action was different from
that used in the battle of Jericho. The spies who
went to view Jericho went right into the city. Ai
also was "viewed," but we do not read that any
spies entered the city. Neither do we hear of another

Rahab, nor of any warning of any kind. The whole procedure was entirely different.

There is a lesson for us in that. The fact that the Lord may have used certain means to achieve certain ends at one time does not mean that He will use the same means and methods elsewhere at another time. There is nothing stereotyped about the ways of God. He has "diversities of operations" (I Cor. 12:6). In each of these battles we may see patterns of His ways. Joshua was to do unto Ai and her king as he had done to Jericho and her king (8:2). But the spoil of Ai, and the cattle thereof they were to take for a prey unto themselves. In the battle of Jericho they were not permitted to share in the spoils. There they did not actually fight. But here, where they themselves went into action, they were allowed to take the prey thereof unto themselves. In so doing, God was not "rectifying a mistake" as some would have us believe. This was a matter of compensation where compensation was due.

The march around Jericho was carried out in broad daylight. Here at Ai the Lord directed Joshua to lay "an ambush for the city behind it." And "so Joshua arose, and *all* the people of war, to go up against Ai." Instead of just three thousand men, as at the first, he chose ten times that number, whom he sent away by night to lie in wait against the city. But Joshua spent the night with that part of the army which was going to feign defeat by fleeing before the men of Ai.

It is very interesting to observe where those who lay in ambush spent the night. It was "between Bethel and Ai, on the west side of Ai" (v. 9), in the very place where Abram had built his altar both before and after his sojourn in Egypt. We may be sure that some reference was made to that that night.

Some may even have recalled that even though
Abram enriched himself in Egypt, he had no altar
while there. At least there is no record of it. In view
of the sad experience through which the Israelites
had passed in connection with Achan, it is not at
all unlikely that some comparisons would be made.
The riches of this world, whether they be of Egypt
or of Jericho, can never enrich the soul.

The mustering of the people in the morning is
also interesting (v. 10). Most of them were placed
on the north side of the city, while an extra five
thousand, as I take it, were sent to reinforce the
ambush on the west side (v. 12). In view of the fact
that there were only twelve thousand men in the
city (v. 25), this is quite remarkable. It shows how
completely they had cast aside their former self-
confidence.

After making all of these arrangements, "Joshua
went that night into the midst of the valley." We
like to think that this is evidence of the humility
of the man. Although he was commander-in-chief,
he went down to a low place. If there is any spiritual
significance in this—and we are inclined to believe
that there is, then we may learn something from
this. Conscious of our weakness, let us humble ourselves under the mighty hand of God that He may
exalt us in due time (I Peter 5:6).

We are not told what Joshua did in the valley
that night. Presumably he was alone. Yet he was not
alone. God was there to strengthen and encourage
His faithful servant.

When daylight came, the king of Ai began the
battle (v. 14). But he knew not that there was an
ambush against him behind the city. To draw him
and his people out of the city, "Joshua and all Israel
made as if they were beaten before them, and fled

by the way of the wilderness (v. 15). But their flight was not a rout. It was all according to plan.

The turning point in this battle came when Joshua, at the command of the Lord, stretched forth the spear that was in his hand toward Ai (v. 18). The spear, a weapon of offense rather than of defense, was used as a signal for the beginning of the offensive and for the ambush to arise and do its part. Joshua did not draw back his hand until he had utterly destroyed all of the inhabitants of Ai (v. 26).

From former experience Joshua knew something of the power of the outstretched hand. He had learned that at Rephidim. It was because Moses' hands were steady till the going down of the sun that Joshua was able to break the power of Amalek and his forces (Exodus 17:12-13). Here he had the opportunity to do for others what Moses had done for him. It may be that we, too, may learn from this to stretch forth our hands in order that others may win victories over the principalities and powers of which these Canaanites are types.

It was not long until the enemy was surrounded and the city burned with fire. The king was taken alive and later hanged on a tree till the evening. Then his body was taken down and cast into the entrance of the gate of the city and covered with stones.

Much of this is very similar to what was done to Achan, but there are differences which are significant. Achan was judged as one of the Lord's people who needed discipline (cf. Acts 5:1-11). But the king of Ai was an enemy of the Lord and His people. Even when it is necessary to deliver a child of God to Satan for the destruction of the flesh (I Cor. 5:5), God's child is so judged in order that his spirit may be saved in the day of the Lord Jesus. The fact that the king of Ai was hanged on a tree shows that his case was different. The Word of God says, "Cursed is every one that hangeth on a tree" (Gal. 3.13). Such a curse was not put on Achan.

Immediately after this we read, "Then Joshua built an altar unto the LORD God of Israel in mount Ebal" (8:30). This was the mount from which the curses of the law were to be read (Deut. 27:13). The location of this altar and the materials used in building it were strictly according to that law. Obedient to the word spoken to him at the beginning of his career as the leader of God's people, Joshua did according to all that was written in the law given by Moses (Joshua 1:8).

We have already seen in our study of chapters 4 and 5 of this book that the Israelites paused prior to the battle of Jericho to erect a memorial of stones taken from the Jordan to renew the rite of circumcision and to celebrate the Passover. The building of the altar in Mount Ebal marks another such pause. Since Joshua was no novice but a seasoned soldier, we may be sure that he did not overlook the military importance of following up his victory at Ai by striking at other important cities. But here we see him recognizing the greater importance of worship and the teaching of the law of Moses.

In the burnt offerings and peace offerings which he offered we observe two aspects of the sacrificial work of our blessed Lord. The former symbolizes the worship which is His due (cf. II Chron. 29: 27-28). By means of it, the offerer gave expression to the praise and worship that was in his heart as he brought to the Lord that which speaks so beautifully of the complete devotion of the Son of God to His Father.

In the peace offering, because the offerer participated in it, we see that which speaks of communion with God. Part of the offering was burned on the altar, and part of it was eaten by the offerer (Lev. 7:15 ff). In that way he enjoyed what God enjoys, and that is the essence of true communion.

In direct connection with this we have the *writing* of the law on the stones, presumably the stones of the altar. If these stones represent the people of God (cf. I Kings 18:31), then we may have here a suggestion of the covenant spoken of in Hebrews 10: 16-17, where we read, "This is the covenant that I will make with them after those days, saith the Lord, I will put my laws into their hearts, and in their minds will I write them; and their sins and iniquities will I remember no more."

Then, as a complement to the writing of the law, there was the reading of the law (8:34). The people were not only to see the law but they were to hear it as well. And the reading was done in the presence of the whole congregation of Israel, with the women and children, and the strangers that lived among them.

In between the verses which tell about the writing of the law and the reading of it, the ark of the covenant is mentioned. This is rather striking because the ark was not mentioned at all in connection with the conquest of Ai. But what we have here would not be complete without it. Thus three important things are brought together in the closing verses of this chapter: First, the altar and the sacrifices which were offered upon it; second, the law written upon the stones of the altar; and last, the ark, within which were the two tables of stone on which that same law was written with the finger of God. But the tables of stone were covered by the mercy seat upon which the blood of atonement was sprinkled, in virtue of which a holy God could meet with His people and commune with them.

It was in the midst of these deeply significant

things that Joshua read the law, all the words of it, "the blessings and the cursing," the pleasant as well as that which was not so pleasant. He did not omit one word. And no one was excused from attending that important meeting. No one was considered too young to hear the Word of God.

When we give God's Word to our children we lay a foundation for the life that now is and for that which is to come. Those of us who had such training in our childhood have cause to be devoutly thankful to God for parents who did not neglect this most important responsibility so that we might know the holy Scriptures which are able to make one wise unto salvation through faith which is in Christ Jesus (II Tim. 3:15).

In this division of the book of Joshua we have seen how God teaches His people lessons in holiness and humility through defeat and discipline. We have also seen that He is able to give His people victory in the very place of defeat.

Then in that which the altar, the ark, and the Book signifies we saw three fundamental things which, if rightly apprehended, will save, sanctify, and strengthen the people of God. The ark, which has the central place here, really signifies God's earthly throne, where He dwelt between the cherubim (Ps. 80:1). Thus did He walk in the midst of them (Deut. 23:14), and therefore they could say with the psalmist, "The LORD of hosts is with us; the God of Jacob is our refuge. Selah" (Ps. 46:7).

CHAPTER NINE

The Battle of Gibeon

(Joshua 9 and 10)

IN THIS PART of the Book of Joshua we have the record of the third great movement in the conquest of Canaan. The first came to a close with the fall of Jericho; the second, with the destruction of Ai. As we have seen, the action against these two cities differed greatly, both in the method of attack, and also in the method of defense. "Jericho was straitly shut up" (Joshua 6:1), but there was no active resistance according to the record. At Ai the Israelites met stiff resistance which they were unable to overcome at the first because of sin in their camp. But when they had purged themselves of that sin, the Lord gave them victory. In this third movement the defenders took the initiative. ". . . they gathered themselves together, to fight with Joshua and with Israel, with one accord" (9:2). It should be pointed out that the kings referred to in verse 1 were little more than city-rulers. That is the reason there were so many in such a small territory. Evidently they were not all of one mind, for "when the inhabitants of Gibeon heard what Joshua had done unto Jericho and Ai, they did work wilily."

We learn from the next chapter that this was an independent move on their part which threw their allies into great confusion. Since we believe these kings to be typical of "principalities and powers" under the control of "the father of lies" we suspect that this was all part of a scheme that was being tried out. The very manner in which they went about this suggests "the wiles of the devil" (Eph. 6:11). What he cannot succeed in doing openly, he will attempt in disguise and by deception. Therefore it will pay us to study his method here, so that we may be aware of "his devices" (II Cor. 2:11).

The Gibeonites feigned themselves to be ambassadors from a far country "and took old sacks upon their asses, and wine bottles, old, and rent, and bound up; and old shoes and clouted upon their feet, and old garments upon them; and all the bread of their provision was dry and mouldy" (9:4-5).

What they brought was *old,* very *old,* for the purpose of substantiating their claim that they had come from a *far* country. Only by convincing the Israelites that they had come from a far country could they expect to make a league with the Israelites.

Evidently the Israelites were suspicious, for they said, "Peradventure ye dwell among us; and how shall we make a league with you?" The question indicates that they had their misgivings. And they did well to be suspicious, because they had been strictly commanded by God to make no covenant with any inhabitant of the land (Exodus 23:32).

Because Joshua suspected that they might not be what they claimed to be, Joshua inquired again, "Who are ye? and from whence come ye?" In reply to the first question they quite humbly referred to themselves as "servants." That reply was polite but rather vague. Their reply to Joshua's second question was equally vague. They merely said that they were from a "very far country" and that they had come a "very long journey." And they had dry, moldy loaves of bread, broken wineskins, and worn-out clothes to prove it! But they presented no documentary evidence. As ambassadors with full power to make a league with another nation, they should have had some authoritative credentials. And the men of Israel made a great mistake in not demanding such credentials. Certainly, their mistake is here recorded for our admonition.

When we hear some supposedly learned man talk about the skeletal remains of prehistoric man, confidently affirming them to be hundreds of thousands of years old, we wonder if we might not compare what he says to the moldy bread of the Gibeonites. At any rate, those of us who have considered such statements in the light of the Word of God must conclude that they are not in the same category with the biblical accounts of man's creation. Scientific books published but a few years ago are out of date now, but the Bible has a living freshness that abides. And the joy that results from feasting on it stands out in happy contrast to the utter joylessness of which the empty and broken wineskins of the Hivites are the symbol.

One wonders how the Israelites could partake of such stale victuals. But "they asked not counsel at the mouth of the LORD" (v. 14). And that is where so many of us fail.

But it did not take the Israelites long to discover their mistake. "It came to pass at the end of three days after they had made a league with them, that they heard that they were their neighbours, and that they dwelt among them" (v. 16).

It appears that the leaders of Israel were responsible for this mistake. "And all the congregation murmured against the princes" (v. 18). But they had "sworn unto them by the LORD God of Israel." Even though they had sworn to their own hurt, they did not alter their word (cf. Psalm 15:4). Whether things would have been different had the common people been consulted, it is hard to say. Since "great

men are not always wise" (Job 32:9), it is important
that we should learn to depend directly on the Lord.
"If any of you lack wisdom, let him ask of God,
that giveth to all men liberally, and upbraideth not;
and it shall be given him" (James 1:5).

THE WISDOM OF THE GIBEONITES

The Gibeonites escaped with their lives, but they
were cursed and reduced to slavery. "Joshua made
them that day hewers of wood and drawers of water
for the congregation, and for the altar of the Lord,
even unto this day, in the place which he should
choose" (9:27). Nevertheless we have to credit
them with wisdom in doing what they did. In some
respects they remind us of the unjust steward whose
master praised him because he had done prudently,
"for the children of this world are in their generation
wiser than the children of light" (Luke 16:8).

In His Sermon on the Mount our Lord said,
"Agree with thine adversary quickly, whiles thou
art in the way with him; lest at any time the adversary deliver thee to the judge, and the judge deliver thee to the officer, and thou be cast into prison.
Verily, I say unto thee, Thou shalt by no means
come out thence, till thou hast paid the uttermost
farthing" (Matt. 5:25).

On another occasion our Lord asked, "What king,
going to make war against another king, sitteth not
down first, and consulteth whether he be able with
ten thousand to meet him that cometh against him
with twenty thousand? Or else, while the other is
yet a great way off, he sendeth an ambassage, and
desireth conditions of peace" (Luke 14:31-32).

Of course, the Lord was not suggesting anything
disingenuous here. Nevertheless, one can see that in
the case of the Gibeonites their actions were not
unlike an embassy seeking terms of peace. Gibeon,

as we shall see, "was a great city, as one of the royal cities." But the inhabitants knew that they could not prevail over Joshua and his armies. Therefore they sought terms of peace, even though they had to take the place of bondmen as a result.

Their primary purpose, so they said, was to save their own lives. They had heard what the Lord did for Israel in Egypt, and what He did to the two kings of the Amorites that were beyond Jordan. It was also told them that the Lord had commanded Moses to give the Israelites all the land, and to destroy all the inhabitants thereof (9:9-10, 24). Evidently they believed that. And for that we must commend them.

Little did they think when they said, "We are thy servants," just how literally that would be true, for servants they became. And yet their service was in one sense a dignified one, because it was for the house of God and for the altar of the Lord, as well as for His people. The psalmist said that he would rather be a doorkeeper in the house of his God, than to dwell in the tents of wickedness (Ps. 84:10). There is no hint in the sacred record that the Gibeonites ever attained to equality with the Israelites. In fact, it is distinctly stated that they "were not of the children of Israel" (II Sam. 21:2). Nevertheless, they were among them (Joshua 10:1).

It was this that worried Adoni-zedec, the king of Jerusalem. He had heard how Joshua had taken Ai and had utterly destroyed it as he had done to Jericho and her king. He had also heard "how the inhabitants of Gibeon made peace with Israel, *and were among them.*" As a result, fear fell upon him and his people, because Gibeon "was greater than Ai, and all the men thereof were mighty." And so he called for help.

Whether or not the kings mentioned in Joshua

10:3-5 are the same as those mentioned in the first
verse of the previous chapter is not clear. Here
only "five kings of the Amorites" are mentioned.
The king of Jerusalem seems to have been their
leader. His name, Adoni-zedec, is rather interesting.
It means, *"lord* of righteousness." It will be recalled
that an earlier king of Jerusalem was called Melchizedek, which means *"king of righteousness"*
(Heb. 7:2). It is quite evident that the two men are
not in the same class, however similar their names
may be. Melchizedek blessed Abram, the great an-
cestor of the Israelites. Adoni-zedec was the very
opposite because he hated the people of God.

Some have seen in Adoni-zedec a type of Anti-
christ, who will one day seat himself "in the temple
of God, showing himself that he is God" (II Thess.
2:4). But we do not have to look that far ahead to
find an illustration of what he may represent. Paul
wrote to the Corinthians that "Satan himself is transformed into an angel of light. Therefore it is no
great thing if his ministers also be transformed as
the *ministers of righteousness* (II Cor. 11:14-15).

As "lord of righteousness," Adoni-zedec may have
argued the justice of his cause in opposing the progress of Joshua and the hosts of Israel. However,
one has but to look into the past record of the
Canaanites to see that they were getting justice.
They were so utterly corrupt that the land itself
vomited out her inhabitants, as stated in Leviticus
18:25.

Adoni-zedec, in his appeal for help, did not claim
to have been attacked by Joshua, or any one else
for that matter. He wanted his allies to come and
help him smite Gibeon because it had made peace
with Joshua and with the children of Israel.

We who have been "delivered . . . from the power
of darkness" (Col. 1:13) know that we also have

to suffer attacks from the wicked one for similar reasons. As long as we were alienated from God and were His enemies in our minds by wicked works, Satan did not disturb us. But the moment we were reconciled to God by Him who made peace through the blood of His cross (Col. 1:20-21), Satan, like Adoni-zedec, assembled his hosts to fight against us. But, thank God, we, like the Gibeonites, may cry to our Joshua for help. He will not fail us.

"So Joshua ascended from Gilgal, he, and all the people of war with him, and all the mighty men of valour" (10:7). Whether this was the Gilgal on the bank of the Jordan, or some other place with the same name, as some suggest, need not detain us. It is the meaning of the name that really matters. It was at Gilgal that the Lord had rolled away the reproach of Egypt from His people. After that they were no longer bondmen, but God's free men. As such, they had nothing to fear.

Accordingly, "the LORD said unto Joshua, Fear them not: for I have delivered them into thine hand; there shall not a man of them stand before thee" (v. 8). This word of encouragement must have been most welcome at this time. The Gibeonites, like the rest of the Canaanites, deserved to be exterminated. The Israelites should never have made a covenant with them, as we have already noted. But mercy glories, or triumphs, over judgment (cf. James 2: 13). And so the Lord did not rebuke His people for what they had done but even encouraged them in their defense of the Gibeonites.

GOD GIVES VICTORY

Thus encouraged, Joshua came upon Adoni-zedec and his allies suddenly, and went up from Gilgal all night. "And the LORD discomfited them before Israel, and slew them with a great slaughter at Gibeon, . . .

and it came to pass, as they fled from before Israel,
. . . that the LORD cast down great stones from
heaven upon them at Azekah, and they died: they
were more which died with hailstones than they
whom the children of Israel slew with the sword"
(vv. 10-11).

In the book of Revelation (16:21) "great hail
out of heaven" is one of the final judgments yet to
be poured out by the Lord upon wicked men. That
which might have descended as a gentle rain, met
by a cold blast, is changed into a deadly hail, dread
symbol of what it means to reject the grace of God.

The victory at Gibeon was celebrated with a
hymn which has occasioned a good deal of contro-
versy. Much depends on what Joshua meant when
he said, "Sun, stand still." Some believe that he was
quoting a bit of poetry. Others look upon the whole
statement as an "inserted passage" which should be
eliminated. Others believe that this should be rendered, "Sun, be silent," that is, "Cease shining."
But the sun did not cease to shine; it "hasted not
to go down about a whole day." That puts the expression in the same category as the familiar expressions, "the sun rises" and "the sun sets," when
we perceive it coming above the horizon or disap-
pearing beyond it. This phenomenom is so common
that we do not generally think of it as a miracle. But
the same One who made the sun and hung it, like
the earth, upon nothing (cf. Job 26:7) could easily
suspend its motion should He so desire. In any
case, "there was no day like that before it or after
it, that the LORD hearkened unto the voice of a man:
for the LORD fought for Israel" (v. 14).

This was one in a series of miracles wrought for
Israel during their conquest of Canaan, such as the
damming of the Jordan and the collapse of the walls
of Jericho. In each of these we get an illustration of

how some particular phase of Satan's power is overcome. By means of the first, an entrance was gained
into his territory. By means of the second, his chief
stronghold was robbed of its defense. By means of
the third, his chief deities, the sun and the moon,
were made to halt when the Lord of all creation
hearkened to the voice of a man and fought for
His people. Together they demonstrate a progressive
victory over Satan and all his hosts.

It appears that the victory at Gibeon was in two
parts, with a brief return to Gilgal between them
(v. 15). The former had to do with the enemies'
hosts in general; the latter, with the execution of
five kings and the smiting of their cities later.

The temporary escape of these five kings from
Joshua merely postponed their judgment. He "sealed
them off," as the saying goes, while he pursued their
armies. When he had made "an end of slaying them
with a very great slaughter," he returned to attend
to their royal masters. He shared his triumph with
the captains of the men of war by inviting them to
put their feet upon the necks of these kings, after
which they were duly executed. In similar vein we
are told that the day is coming when the God of
peace shall bruise Satan under our feet (Rom. 16:
20) in fulfillment of the promise made in the garden
of Eden that the woman's Seed would bruise the
serpent's head. In that day we shall triumph in His
triumphs!

THE RIGHT MEASURE

As each city was destroyed, it became the measure
of the next victory. Makkedah seems to be the only
exception to this rule, but its destruction is compared
with that of Jericho, which set the standard, as it
were. The destruction of Libnah set the standard for
Lachish. The king of Gezer came to the help of

Lachish, but he was destroyed in the attempt. So little is made of this, however, that it seems to be quite incidental.

The destruction of Eglon, in turn, became the measure of that which overtook Hebron. Finally, the destruction of Debir is measured by that which overtook Hebron and Libnah.

This measuring of each victory by the one immediately preceding it may teach us a lesson. Most of us are prone to measure what we do by something that was done years ago. No doubt there are times when that is perfectly in order. But there should be in every Christian's life a succession of victories, each becoming a standard for the next.

"So Joshua smote all the country of the hills, and of the south, and of the vale, and of the springs, and all their kings" (v. 40). What a variety of terrain we see here! Joshua and his armies achieved victories in the rugged mountains and in the low spots; by refreshing springs and in the desert. A good soldier is ready for any kind of terrain.

Joshua was thorough in what he did. "He left none remaining." Joshua did according to all that he had been commanded. Saul, years later, is seen in sharp contrast to Joshua. We read that Saul "spared Agag, and the best of the sheep, and of the oxen, and of the fatlings, and the lambs, and all that was good, and would not utterly destroy them" (I Sam. 15), even though he had been commanded to do so.

It is quite remarkable to find in the brief summary here the name of the very place where Israel might have entered the land some thirty-eight years before (v. 41). Joshua, as one of the twelve spies whom Moses sent to spy out the land, must have known the territory from "Kadesh-barnea even to

Gaza" very well. "And all these kings and their land did Joshua take at one time, because the LORD God of Israel fought for Israel."

As we come to the close of another phase of the conquest of Canaan, we see that it is appropriately marked by a return to Gilgal, which seems to have been their base of operations. Every soldier of Jesus Christ needs such a base. Thank God, we have it in "a place called Calvary," where the Lord Jesus did for us what Gilgal signified to the Israelite. God forbid that we should glory in our victories over the enemy. Rather let us glory in the cross of our Lord Jesus Christ, by whom the world is crucified unto us, and we unto the world.

CHAPTER TEN

The Battle of Lake Merom

(Joshua 11 and 12)

WE COME NOW to the fourth, and last, stage of the conquest of the land of Canaan under the leadership of Joshua. Its beginnings resemble those of the third campaign in that there was a gathering of several powers united to fight against Israel. But this force outnumbered any that Joshua and his men of war had had to face before.

Josephus says that the confederate forces amounted to 300,000 foot soldiers, 10,000 cavalry, and 20,000 war chariots. And the Scripture says that "they went out, they and all their hosts with them, much people, even as the sand that is upon the sea shore in multitude, with horses and chariots very many" (Joshua 11:14). Jabin, king of Hazor, took the lead in all of this, "for Hazor beforetime was the head of all those kingdoms" (v. 10).

Not all of the places mentioned in the first three verses of this chapter have been positively identified as yet. But their general location seems to have been in the region which we know as Galilee. The mention of Chinneroth, which gave its name to the Sea of Chinnereth (Num. 34:11), and from which the name Gennesaret is derived (Luke 5:1), gives us a very definite clue. And the expression "under [or, at the foot of] Hermon in the land of Mizpeh" (Joshua 11:3) seems to confirm the view that this is "Galilee of the nations."

In this region lies one of the world's most famous battlefields, the plain of Esdraelon, or "the place called in the Hebrew tongue Armageddon" (Rev. 16:16). It was the scene of two great victories for Israel: that of Barak over the Canaanites and that of Gideon over the Midianites (Judges 4:16; 5:19).

It was also the scene of three disasters: the death of Saul and Jonathan (I Samuel 31), the death of Amaziah (II Kings 9:27), and the death of Josiah (II Kings 23:29). The last of these, sometimes called "the sunset of the Jewish kingdom," is referred to by the prophet Zechariah in connection with the future restoration of Israel. "In that day there shall be a great mourning in Jerusalem, as the mourning of Hadadrimmon in the valley of Megiddon" (Zechariah 12:11). "That day," of course, is the day when they shall look upon Him whom they pierced and when they shall mourn for Him as one mourneth for his only son, and be in bitterness for Him as one that is in bitterness for his firstborn.

It will also be the rallying-place of "the kings of the whole earth and of the whole world" when they gather "together into a place called in the Hebrew tongue Armageddon" for "the battle of that great day of God Almighty." It is quite possible that the battle which took place there in Joshua's day was a foreshadowing of that great event.

This battle was not unforeseen because the Lord had said this years before, "When thou goest out to battle against thine enemies, and seest horses, and chariots, and a people more than thou, be not afraid of them: for the LORD thy God is with thee" (Deut. 20:1). In like manner He said to Joshua, "Be not afraid of them: for to morrow about this time I will deliver them up all slain before Israel: thou shalt hough their horses, and burn their chariots with fire (Joshua 11:6).

The battle was brief indeed. In less than twenty-four hours the once formidable array was turned into a rout. In a few brief sentences we get the story of their ignominious defeat (vv. 7-9). "And Joshua did unto them as the LORD bade him; he houghed their horses, and burnt their chariots with fire."

Such references to horses and chariots are very interesting. This particular reference marks the first time that horses and chariots are mentioned in connection with the conquest of Canaan. The hamstringing of the horses and the destruction of the chariots was not without reason. They were used by the Canaanites not only in warfare but also in their idolatrous worship. No king of Israel was to "multiply horses to himself, nor cause the people to return to Egypt, to the end that he should multiply horses: forasmuch as the LORD hath said unto you, Ye shall henceforth return no more that way" (Deut. 17:16). The Lord wants His people to trust in Him and not in horses and chariots (cf. Ps. 20:7).

How utterly Israel disregarded all of this is seen in their later history. When Josiah came to the throne, the kings of Judah had actually given horses "to the sun, at the entering of the house of the Lord" (II Kings 23:11). Josiah not only removed these but he also "burned the chariots of the sun with fire."

In view of all of this, it is easy to see why the Lord commanded Joshua to destroy the horses and chariots of the Gentiles. He would not have them rely on such things for victory, nor give them a place in the worship of the true God. But men are prone to worship that which brings them success. "They sacrifice unto their net, and burn incense unto their drag: because by them their portion is fat, and their meat plenteous (Hab. 1:16). To some the destruction of these horses and chariots may have looked like needless waste. But nothing is wasted which is destroyed in order that we may be saved from spiritual disaster.

After Joshua had utterly destroyed these things he "turned back, and took Hazor, and smote the king thereof with the sword: . . . and they smote all the souls that were therein with the edge of the sword, . . . and he burnt Hazor with fire" (11:10-11). No doubt Hazor was totally destroyed because it was the headquarters of that league of wicked nations whom God was then judging because of their great wickedness.

In so doing, Joshua was merely obeying orders. He did as the Lord bade him (v. 9), and "as the LORD commanded Moses his servant, so did Moses command Joshua, and so did Joshua (v. 15). "And all the cities of those kings, and all the kings of them, did Joshua take, and smote them with the edge of the sword, and he utterly destroyed them, as Moses the servant of the LORD commanded" (v. 12).

But there were some exceptions. "As for the cities that stood still in their strength, Israel burned none of them" (v. 13). The American Standard Version, in common with some other translations, renders this: "The cities that stood on their mounds, Israel burned none of them, save Hazor only: that did Joshua burn." That which was typical of "Satan's seat" was totally destroyed. The other cities were spared, so it seems, in order that they might glorify the Lord in and through their redeemed inhabitants.

We find a rather striking reference to this part of the land in Isaiah 9:1-2, where it is said of "Galilee of the nations" that "the people that walked in darkness have seen a great light: they that dwell in the land of the shadow of death, upon them hath the light shined." According to Matthew 4:13-15 this was fulfilled when our Lord took up His residence in Capernaum. We marvel that He would choose to live in a place like that. In so doing He was exalting it to heaven (Matt. 11:23). But He also predicted that it would be brought down to hell! For "this is the condemnation, that light is come into the world, and men loved darkness rather than light, because their deeds were evil (John 3:19).

Since the deeds of the Canaanites were evil, "it was of the LORD to harden their hearts, that they should come against Israel in battle, that he might destroy them utterly, and that they might have no favour, but that he might destroy them, as the LORD commanded Moses" (11:20). They were warned when the Lord destroyed Sodom and Gomorrah in Abraham's day. They had also heard of what He did to the two kings of the Amorites on the other side of the Jordan. But none of the Canaanites sought peace with Israel except the inhabitants of Gibeon.

The hardening of their hearts was punitive. Their iniquity was now full (cf. Gen. 15:16). The long respite granted to them by a long-suffering God wrought no repentance in them. According to their hardness and impenitence they treasured up unto themselves wrath against the day of wrath and revelation of the righteous judgment of God (cf. Rom. 2:4-5).

Among the enemies with whom Joshua had to deal at this time were the Anakim, "a people great and tall," of whom it was said, "Who can stand before the children of Anak!" (Deut. 9:2). Evidently they were considered invincible. But we read that "Joshua destroyed them utterly with their cities. There was none of the Anakims left in *the land of the children of Israel*" (Joshua 11:21-22).

It is of interest to note that this is the first time that the land is referred to in this way. And since the land is so described in connection with the extermination of the giants, it looks as though Israel's actual possession of the land depended on this. But there were still giants in the land of the Philistines—in Gaza, Gath, and Ashdod. It was from Gath that Goliath came to defy the armies of the living God in David's day. But he was no match for one who came to him in the name of the Lord of hosts (cf. I Sam. 17:45).

This should be an encouragement to us, for greater is He that is in us than he that is in the world (I John 4:4). Therefore it matters not how strong and powerful the enemy may be, "We are more than conquerors through him that loved us" (Rom. 8:37).

RECAPITULATION

"So Joshua took the whole land, according to all that the LORD said unto Moses; and Joshua gave it for an inheritance unto Israel according to their divisions by their tribes. And the land rested from war" (Joshua 11:23).

The chapter which follows gives a summary of what had been accomplished thus far. It is very interesting to note that the Lord credits His people with having done things which, as a matter of fact, He had done Himself. It was He who smote their foes, and it was He who gave them the land. But here we read, "Now these are the kings of the land, which the children of Israel smote, and possessed their land" (12:1).

The conquest actually began before they crossed the Jordan, and the first part of this chapter gives us a brief account of that. It has to do particularly with what Moses, the servant of the Lord, did and

with the land which he gave "for a possession unto
the Reubenites, and the Gadites, and the half tribe
of Manasseh (v. 6). The latter part of the chapter
recounts the victories won by Joshua, and gives a
brief description of the territory which he "gave unto
the tribes of Israel for a possession" (vv. 7-8).

In this chapter we also get a list of the thirty-one
kings of the country which Joshua and the children
of Israel smote "on this side Jordan on the west."
No doubt a story could have been told about each
one of these. But it was not necessary to go into detail. Enough detail is given us in connection with
the battles of Jericho, Ai, Gibeon, and the one "at
the waters of Merom," to enable us to imagine what
went on in the other battles also.

One is impressed with the large number of kings
in such a small country. Such division of power
usually results in weakness. But in this case common hatred, as well as common fear, would serve
to unite people who otherwise would be at variance
with each other. We have a classic example of such
a union in Luke 23:12, where we read that "the
same day Pilate and Herod were made friends together: for before they were at enmity between
themselves." It was their attitude toward the Lord
Jesus that united them.

Thank God, Christians enjoy a unity that the
world knows nothing about. In spite of many out-
ward divisions, there is an inner "unity of the Spirit"
(Eph. 4:3) because "by one Spirit are we all baptized into one body, whether we be Jews or Gentiles,
whether we be bond or free; and have been all made
to drink into one Spirit (I Cor. 12:13).

It is our responsibility to endeavor "to keep the
unity of the Spirit in the bond of peace." Disintegra-
tion is manifest everywhere. But this can be overcome by a common occupation with Christ and

united submission to His authority in all things. Thus may we possess our possessions, and give thanks to Him who giveth us the victory through our Lord Jesus Christ.

CHAPTER ELEVEN

Possessing the Land

(Joshua 13-15)

JOSHUA IS ONE of six persons referred to in Scripture as "old and stricken in years." The others are Abraham and Sarah, David, and Zacharias and Elisabeth, the parents of John the Baptist. With the exception of David, all of these were at the point of realizing their dearest hopes when this was said of them. Life's greatest achievements were just ahead of them. As for Joshua, he was told, "There remaineth yet very much land to be possessed." He had won many battles and conquered many nations. But his work was far from finished. He had been commissioned not only to *conquer* but also to *divide* the land for an inheritance. After that it was up to the Israelites to actually possess it.

The frequent repetition of the little word "all" in chapter 13 is intended, no doubt, to impress us with the fact that nothing short of complete possession was in the mind of the Lord for His people. The expressions *"all* the borders of the Philistines" (v. 2), and *"all* the land of the Canaanites" (v. 4), emphasize that. "This is the land that yet remaineth."

It is interesting to note that all the borders of the Philistines head the list here. The Philistines were bitter enemies of God's ancient people. From Genesis 10:13-14 it would appear that they were related to the Egyptians, and were descendants of Ham, the son of Noah. The name of the country they lived in, Philistia, means "the land of wanderers." And the

road by which they traveled to and from Egypt was
known as "the way of the Philistines" (Exodus
13:17), a shortcut when compared with the route
the Israelites had to take. Thus, as another has said,
they represent "natural men come into spiritual
blessing, not by the power of God, but in a natural
way." In due time they gave their name to the whole
land. Philistia is the same as Palestine.

Our chapter also speaks about "all the land of
the Canaanites" (v. 4). According to good authority,
a Canaanite is a "merchant," or a "trafficker." It
so happens that the word "merchant" in Hosea 12:7
is "Canaan" in the original. "He is a merchant
[Canaan], the balances of deceit are in his hand: he
loveth to oppress."

If the Philistines represent those who come into
spiritual blessings without a spiritual regeneration,
the Canaanites may serve as an example of those
who traffic in the things of God without having
experienced them. All such must be overcome and
dispossessed if the Lord's people are to possess their
possessions. But it is not easy to dislodge them. "All
the inhabitants of the hill country," that is, those
who occupy high places, as it were, will oppose every
effort to expel them.

But it is in this very connection that the Lord
says, "Them will I drive out from before the children of Israel" (13:6). Note that He did not say
that He would drive them out *for* the children of
Israel, but "from *before*" them. In the nature of
things, this would require their involvement. Thus
they would share not only in the victory but in the
winning of it.

The actual division of the land was to be by lot.
But since the whole disposing of the lot was of the
Lord (Prov. 16:33), each one's portion was divinely
determined. In Acts 1:24-26 we note that the cast-

ing of the lot was preceded by prayer. And we like to believe that that was customary. This was no mere game of chance but a divinely appointed method of procedure, and the results were final.

We are not told here whether this method was used in assigning the territories east of the Jordan where the tribes of Reuben and Gad, and the half tribe of Manasseh, received their inheritance. But see Joshua 17:1. Here we are simply told that they "received their inheritance, which Moses gave them, beyond Jordan eastward" (v. 8). This inheritance is given considerable notice in the verses which follow, in which we find both encouragement and warning. The fact that some were already in possession of their inheritance must have served as an incentive to the rest to claim theirs also.

Evidently some of the Israelites were satisfied with less than their full portion. We read that the "children of Israel expelled not the Geshurites, nor the Maachathites; but the Geshurites and the Maachathites dwell among the Israelites until this day" (13:13). This imcomplete possession, this failure to possess *all* their inheritance was evidently due to lack of faith and courage on the part of the Israelites. Had they gone forward against their foes, the Lord would have driven them out from before them, as He said. Many an enemy is thus allowed to dwell among the people of God because they do not have the faith and courage to take Him at His word, and to move forward.

But there was success as well as failure. And the same Spirit who tells us of the failures is careful to tell us of the successes also. "All the cities of the plain, and all the kingdom of Sihon . . . Moses smote with the princes of Midian . . . which were dukes of Sihon, dwelling in the country" (13:21). There is one enemy who comes in for special mention: Balaam, the son of Beor, the soothsayer. He is actually mentioned three times in the New Testament. In II Peter 2:15 we read of "the way of Balaam"; in Jude 11, of "the error of Balaam"; and in Revelation 2:14, of "the doctrine of Balaam."

Balaam was a man who loved the reward of unrighteousness, and he taught Balak to cast a snare before the sons of Israel, to eat of idol sacrifices and to commit fornication. One is not surprised, therefore, to read that the children of Israel slew him with the sword. And yet, some of his utterances, as recorded in Numbers 23 and 24, are among the most sublime in the Bible. But that goes to show how conversant one may be with divine things and yet be an apostate, willing to curse the people of God for material gain. What a warning there is here for those who may be tempted to "run greedily" after his error.

NO LAND FOR THE LEVITES

In beautiful contrast, we now see the tribe of Levi to whom Moses, himself a member of that tribe, "gave none inheritance; the sacrifices of the LORD God of Israel made by fire are their inheritance, as he said unto them" (13:14). It goes without saying that their having no inheritance was not because there was no more land for them. Very much land remained to be possessed. However, they did receive cities to dwell in (14:4), including the cities of refuge. Thus the Levites were evenly distributed through the whole of the land. But there was no particular province which they could call their own.

The inheritance of the Levites was better than anything else that might have been given them. By taking into account the spiritual significance of the offerings which they inherited (cf. Lev. 1—7), we see how rich they really were. Every aspect of the

work of Christ may be seen in those offerings. Thus
they could know Him not only as the sin and trespass offering, but also as the peace offering, which
speaks of communion with God because part of it
was burned on the altar, and part was eaten by the
offerer. The burnt offering, which was totally consumed upon the altar, speaks of our Lord's complete devotion and dedication to the will of His
Father. Jut how fully the priests and Levites entered
into all of this we do not know.

But the tribe of Levi got even more than this.
From the last verse of chapter 13 we learn that the
Lord God of Israel Himself was to be their inheritance. It is a blessed thing to know something about
the work of Christ, but it is even more blessed to
know Him (cf. Phil. 3:10). Our knowledge of the
work of Christ should lead us to a deeper appreciation of Him. Failure to grow in appreciation of
Christ Himself indicates a sad lack in one's spiritual
life. The person and work of Christ are among the
most precious themes in the Bible. It is right that
we should appreciate the work of Christ because it
is by that that we are saved. But how much we miss,
and how we grieve Him, if we are content to know
only what He did for us. We are to "grow in grace,
and in the knowledge of our Lord and Saviour Jesus
Christ" (II Peter 3:18).

To give completeness to the theme now before us,
let us anticipate a bit and consider Joshua 18:7,
where we find another reference to the inheritance of
the Levites. "The priesthood of the LORD is their
inheritance." Now, the application of this to ourselves may seem to be presumptuous. It was not
difficult to see how the various sacrifices typify
different aspects of the work of our Blessed Lord,
all of which we may appropriate by faith. Then, too,
we can see how He Himself is given to us to satisfy

our hearts' deepest longings. But the priesthood! Who but "the clergy" could claim that?

When we turn to I Peter 2, however, we discover that those who are likened to newborn babes in the family of God, are also said to be a holy and a royal priesthood—a holy priesthood (v. 5) to offer up spiritual sacrifices which are acceptable to God by Jesus Christ, and a royal priesthood (v. 9), whose function it is to show forth the virtues of Him who called them out of darkness into His marvelous light. Thus we see how Levi's inheritance is a perfect type of our own.

The abiding character of these offerings is indicated in Ezekiel 44:28-30, from which we learn that the offerings to be presented in the millenium are still said to be the inheritance of the priests. Speaking of the sin offering in particular, (v. 27) the Lord says, "It shall be unto them for an inheritance" (v. 28). And then, in direct connection, He adds, "I am their inheritance: and ye shall give them no possession in Israel: I am their possession." The word for "possession" is said to include the idea of permanence. According to one authority it means "what is held fast." God, who never changes, becomes the eternal portion of His people. Blessed be the God and Father of our Lord Jesus Christ who has so richly blessed us!

GOD'S REWARD FOR FAITHFULNESS

The next thing to claim our attention is the order in which the tribes inherited. The first to obtain an inheritance in the land was the royal tribe of Judah, the tribe whose name had been brought into disrepute by Achan, the troubler of Israel. It is refreshing to find in this chapter the name of Caleb, who brought honor to the tribe of Judah. Whereas

Achan had his heart set on worldly things, Caleb wholly followed the Lord.

For forty-five years Caleb had cherished the hope of possessing the very ground on which he walked when he went to spy out the land with Joshua and the other spies. Only he and Joshua remained of that group now, the others having forfeited the privilege of entering in because of their unbelief and the evil report which they brought back.

Caleb's link with Joshua is interesting. Together they remind one of other prominent pairs of men who are mentioned in the Bible, such as David and Jonathan, and Paul and Silas. Caleb may not have had the qualifications for leadership with which his distinguished colleague was so rarely gifted, but he was a man of strong courage and unflagging perseverance.

Apparently Caleb was given the privilege of choosing his own inheritance, within the boundaries of Judah's lot. His companion Joshua seems to have been the only other individual to whom that privilege was granted (cf. Joshua 19:49-50).

It may be in order here to inquire why Caleb wanted Hebron for his inheritance. We recall that Hebron was Abram's choice after he returned from his sojourn in Egypt, and after Lot had separated from him. It was at that time that the Lord invited Abram to walk through the land according to the length of it and the breadth of it. "Then Abram removed his tent, and came and dwelt in the plain of Mamre, which is in Hebron, and built there an altar unto the LORD" (Gen. 13:18). Neither Egypt with all of its riches, nor yet the well-watered plain of Jordan attracted the patriarch. Hebron was his choice. And it was Caleb's choice also.

It was from Hebron that Joseph set out to see how his brethren fared (Gen. 37:14), never to re-

turn until he came there to bury his father Jacob
(Gen. 50:12-14). Abraham and Sarah, as well as
Isaac and Rebecca, were buried there. And there
Jacob buried Leah. It was truly a place of tombs.
But it was also a place of hallowed memories. Moreover, it was a city of refuge, a distinction which
even Jerusalem did not have. It was there that David
reigned for the first seven years of his reign. This
was the spot which Caleb desired to possess.

VIGOR IN OLD AGE

At that time the Anakim were in possession, and
the city bore the name of Kirjath-arba, or city of
Arba, the father of Anak, whose three sons Caleb
dispossessed (Joshua 15:13-14). Caleb was not
looking for a soft spot, even though he was then
eighty-five years old. Forty-five years of desert life
did not weaken him in the least. The Lord had sus-
tained him with resources which were supernatural.
Then, too, the very thought of possessing Hebron
must have made the toils of the road seem as nothing. Evidently the joy of the Lord was his strength.
That was the secret of his perseverance. He stands
out in bright contrast to Solomon, who did evil in
the sight of the Lord and did not wholly follow Him
(I Kings 11:6).

Caleb believed the word of God. Said he to
Joshua, "Thou knowest the thing that the LORD said
unto Moses the man of God concerning me and thee
in Kadesh-barnea" (14:6). He also reminded
Joshua that he had brought back an honest report
after spying out the land, as it was in his heart
(v. 7). Yes, his heart was in it. When others, by
their evil report, made the heart of the people to
melt with fear, he wholly followed the Lord his
God (v. 8).

But he claimed no glory for himself. It was the

Lord who had kept him alive all those years, and it was because of His blessing and care that he was as strong at eighty-five as he had been at forty. And that accounts for the request which he made. "Now therefore give me this mountain, whereof the LORD spake in that day; for thou heardest in that day how the Anakims were there, and that the cities were great and fenced: if so be the LORD will be with me, then I shall be able to drive them out, as the LORD said" (v. 12).

We are not surprised, therefore, that Joshua blessed him and gave him his heart's desire. "Hebron therefore became the inheritance of Caleb the son of Jephunneh the Kenezite unto this day, because he wholly followed the LORD God of Israel" (v. 14.) After that it was no longer known as the city of Arba, chief of the Anakim but as Hebron, the city of "the friend of God." "And the land had rest from war" (v. 15).

ENEMIES ON THE BORDER

Having dealt at some length with the inheritance of Caleb, the Spirit of God now takes up the inheritance of the tribe of Judah as a whole, with respect to its borders and its topography. The names of its borders reveal something of the character of their near neighbors.

To begin with, there was "the border of Edom" (Joshua 15:1). The books of Numbers and Deuteronomy show how the Edomites hated the children of Israel. So also does the book of Obadiah. In view of this we may be sure that "the border of Edom" suggests nothing friendly.

Then there was "the shore of the salt sea" (v. 2), otherwise known as the Dead Sea. This part of the land was known as "the wilderness of Judah," where David wrote Psalm 63. The first verse of that psalm tells what it was like. The south border extended to "the river of Egypt" (v. 4), beyond which lay the "house of bondage" from which Israel had been delivered by divine power. We may be sure the people of God had no friends there.

The east border stretched along the Salt Sea right up to the mouth of the Jordan, or "the uttermost part of Jordan" (v. 5). This was close to the place where the Israelites crossed the river.

The places mentioned in the next few verses are quite different from those already considered. "The stone of Bohan the son of Reuben" (15:6) was probably a memorial of some sort. It is mentioned again in Joshua 18:17 and appears to have been an important landmark. Whether it was to serve as an encouragement, or as a warning, we do not know. One thing is certain, it marked a turning point.

"And the border went up toward Debir" (v. 7). The older name of Debir was Kirjath-sepher, which means "the city of the book." Although this border was *toward* Debir, it was *from* the valley of Achor. How good it is when our path leads *from* the valley of trouble *to* the Word of God, and *looks toward* Gilgal, where the reproach of Egypt was rolled away. Deep spiritual lessons may be learned from such simple things.

And so we might go on and find significance in every word here. "The south side of the river" and the border passing "toward the waters of En-shemesh" (v. 7) suggests refreshing stops where otherwise we might see only hard lines defining the legal limits of our inheritance. When we are tempted to think that we are being fenced in by something we have read in the Word concerning our conduct as children of God, let us think on the refreshing experiences of life signified by "the waters of En-shemesh."

EVERY ADVANCE IS CHALLENGED

Sometimes the Lord's path for us takes us through places that are somber indeed. The next verse in our chapter furnishes us with an illustration of this. "The border went up by the valley of the son of Hinnom," the well-known site of horrible heathen practices. It may be that we need to go by this valley in order that we may learn to appreciate what we have been saved from.

But this is not the only valley that we have to pass in this way. We have already been to the valley of Achor. Now we come to the valley of the giants (v. 8), the base of powerful forces which challenge every advance we may make in the things of God. But nothing can stop a soul that is moving on with God. The path takes us from fountain to fountain, and from mountain to mountain. The border takes us through the country of the Philistines (v. 11) and terminates at the Great Sea (v. 12). The road is not monotonous. Its topographical features are just as interesting as its geographical details. And in them we believe that we can detect faint shadows of the "inheritance incorruptible, and undefiled, and that fadeth not away, reserved in heaven for you" (I Peter 1:4).

Such an inheritance should have moved many to go in and really possess their possessions. But, as always, certain individuals had to take the lead. But a good leader also knows how to incite others to action and participation.

Caleb was such a leader. When he said, "He that smiteth Kirjath-sepher [the city of the book], and taketh it, to him will I give Achsah my daughter to wife," his nephew Othniel [lion of God] took it. And Caleb "gave him Achsah his daughter to wife" (vv. 16-17). This fact is recorded twice in the Bible,

here and in Judges 1:12-13. In Scripture this type of
repetition is significant. It is as if the Lord would
emphasize the wonderful influence one noble soul
may have upon another.

But the story does not end there. In Achsah we
see some of the traits of her father. First of all, we
note how she urged Othniel "to ask of her father a
field." But when she herself was asked what she desired, she replied, "Give me a blessing; for thou
hast given me a south land; give me also springs of
water" (vv. 18-19). What blessed dissatisfaction! We
are not told whether this was her wedding present.
One thing is clear; she wanted that which would
make the south land fruitful. She wanted not an
exchange but an addition.

So her father "gave her the upper springs, and
the nether springs." In the former we may see a
suggestion of the heavenly sources of all true blessing. "Every good gift and every perfect gift is from
above, and cometh down from the Father of lights,
with whom is no variableness, neither shadow of
turning" (James 1:17). The lower springs, on the
other hand, suggest those sources of refreshment
which require us to bow down and to humble ourselves in order that we may enjoy them. We need
both, and our blessed Lord provides both. Our lot
here below may appear to be a barren southland.
But all our springs are in Him (Ps. 87:7). "He
turneth the wilderness into a standing water, and
dry ground into watersprings" (Ps. 107:35).

Such was the influence of Caleb who chose
Hebron (said to mean "communion") in preference
to all else that the land had to offer. To him Hebron,
which speaks of communion with God, was far more
attractive than the vineyards of Eschol with its
grapes, pomegranates, and figs (Num. 13:23). To
him, Hebron was worth all of the years of patient

toil and waiting in the desert, as well as the fighting in the land itself. The sons of Anak were no match for a man like that, even though they outnumbered him three to one.

But the preparation for victory over these giants was made in the years prior to that time. It took courage to differ with the report of the majority at Kadesh-barnea. It required will power to resist the temptation to settle down on the east of Jordan as some had done. Such early victories over self fitted him to win victories over others later.

Caleb seems to have been the only one who drove out *all* his enemies, something that could not be said for the rest of the tribe of Judah. They did not drive out the Jebusites. Consequently they had to dwell with them at Jerusalem.

Caleb took complete possession of that for which he had fought so courageously and successfully. "He wholly followed the Lord God of Israel." God give us more such men—men who are ready to endure hardness as good soldiers of Jesus Christ; men who will "be strong in the Lord, and in the power of his might" (Eph. 6:10).

CHAPTER TWELVE

The Portion of Joseph

(Joshua 16 and 17)

THE FIRST FOUR VERSES of Joshua 16 deal with that
which is common to both the sons of Joseph. "The
children of Joseph were two tribes, Manasseh and
Ephraim (14:4). These two sons were born unto
Joseph "before the years of famine came" in Egypt
(Gen. 41:50). Their mother was "Asenath the
daughter of Poti-pherah priest of On." Evidently she
was an Egyptian. But the paternal grandmother of
Manasseh and Ephraim was none other than the
beloved Rachel. And their father, Joseph, was
Rachel's firstborn. Their inheritance in the land was
determined by lot, the whole disposing of which was
of the Lord (Prov. 16:33).

In the prophecy concerning Jacob's sons we find
that Jacob said a good deal more about Judah and
Joseph than he did about any of the others. Concerning the latter, from whom Joshua descended, he
said, "Joseph is a fruitful bough, even a fruitful
bough by a well; whose branches run over the wall"
(Gen. 49:22). In the passage now before us, we
read that the first turning point in Joseph's border
was at "the water of Jericho on the east." No doubt
these words refer to the spring which was healed
in the days of the prophet Elisha, who "cast salt
in there," saying, "Thus saith the LORD, I have
healed these waters; there shall not be from thence
any more death or barren land" (II Kings 2:21).

It would seem that the "water of Jericho" was sweet originally, and that its bitterness in the days of Elisha was the result of the judgment poured out upon Jericho in the days of Joshua. In keeping with that, the next location mentioned here is "the wilderness that goeth up from Jericho." But unpromising as these beginnings appear to be, they lead to Bethel, which Jacob described as "none other but the house of God" and "the gate of heaven" (Gen. 28:17-19).

The directions which the border takes are indicated by the words "goeth up" (v. 1), "goeth out" and "passeth along" (v. 2), "goeth down westward" (v. 3), and "goings out [or end] . . . at the sea" (v. 3). All of the ups and downs of life may find illustration here. There is no monotony; on the contrary, there is a delightful variety. When "the children of Joseph, Manasseh and Ephraim, took their inheritance" (v. 4), they received it, or, took possession of it. Evidently they were satisfied with their lot. And well they might, because, for the most part, it included the "pleasant country lying in the midst of western Palestine" (Lange).

Having considered that which was common to both the sons of Joseph (vv. 1-4), we come to that which pertained to each in particular. But now the natural order is reversed and Ephraim is placed before Manasseh, even though the latter was the older of the two. It was their grandfather, Jacob, who first reversed the natural order. In bringing the lads to Israel to receive his blessing, Joseph put Ephraim toward Israel's left hand, and Manasseh toward his right hand. But Israel guided his hands wittingly and "set Ephraim before Manasseh." In so doing he was acting on a principle established by the Lord Himself when He placed Jacob before Esau. In this we may see a foreshadowing of the future eminence of Ephraim (Gen. 48:19-20). Ephraim is said to mean "double fruit." We recall that our Lord said, "Herein is my Father glorified, that ye bear much fruit" (John 15:8). Since the name Manasseh means "forgetting" (Gen. 41:51), it may be that we have here a negative and a positive; with precedence given to the positive.

In Joshua 16:9 we read, "The *separate* cities for the children of Ephraim were *among* the inheritance of the children of Manasseh." Separate, and yet among! The two brethren had much in common, but they also had things which were special and distinct.

"Manasseh had the land of Tappuah: but Tappuah on the border of Manasseh belonged to the children of Ephraim" (Joshua 17:8). "The coast of Manasseh also was on the north side of the river, and the outgoings of it were at the sea: southward it was Ephraim's, and northward it was Manasseh's, and the sea is his border" (vv. 9-10). The river served as a dividing line between their inheritances, but both could use it as a source of refreshment. The one had access to it from the south side, and the other from the north. The point of view was different, but the stream served both alike.

In like manner, the Holy Spirit, whom our Lord likened to "rivers of living water" (John 7:38-39), is a common source of refreshment for all God's people. And in I Corinthians 12:13 we read that "by one Spirit are we all baptized into one body, whether we be Jews or Gentiles, whether we be bond or free; and have been all made to drink into one Spirit." In the Church "there are diversities of gifts, but the same Spirit. And there are differences of administrations, but the same Lord. And there are diversities of operations, but it is the same God which worketh all in all" (I Cor. 12:4-6).

We find another example of fellowship in Joshua

17:11, where we read of certain cities which "Manasseh had in Issachar and Asher." We have seen that Ephraim had cities among those of Manasseh. Here we see how Manasseh, in turn, inherits cities among those of Issachar and Asher. This intermingling and overlapping is both interesting and instructive. The inheritance of each tribe was distinct, and yet they were inseparable. What a lesson for us today!

Another beautiful thing in this passage is the case of the daughters of Zelophehad (17:3). These women evidently feared that because they had no brothers they might be overlooked or ignored in the distribution of the inheritance to which they were entitled. Anticipating this they had actually taken up the matter with Moses long before they got into the land. Although they belonged to the so-called "weaker sex" they were determined to obtain their rightful portion. The Lord had commanded Moses to give them an inheritance among their brethren. "Therefore according to the commandment of the LORD he gave them an inheritance among the brethren of their father" (v. 4). They took the Lord at His word, and He honored their faith.

In dark contrast to the determination of these women, the Ephraimites showed a lack of determination in securing their entire inheritance. We read that "they drove not out the Canaanites that dwelt in Gezer: but the Canaanites dwell among the Ephraimites unto this day, and serve under tribute" (16:10). This part of the country has been described as "the fairest portion of the land of Palestine" (J. Lloyd). No wonder the Canaanites wanted to stay! And they did stay. But they should have been driven out. The fact that they were not driven out manifests weakness, or worse, on the part of the Lord's people.

It is true that the Canaanites were made to "serve

under tribute," that is, they were reduced to slavery, but that could never compensate for complete victory over them. How easily, at times, we sacrifice victory for tribute. Alas, there are many whose souls are saved, but whose lives are lost, all for the sake of some worldly gain.

The children of Manasseh were no better than the sons of Ephraim in this respect, for it is said of them that they "could not drive out the inhabitants of those cities; but the Canaanites would dwell in that land" (17:12). And the sons of Ephraim thus failed in spite of the fact that one of their brethren was "Machir the firstborn of Manasseh, the father of Gilead," and "he was a man of war" (17:1). But Machir was already in possession of "Gilead and Bashan," on the east of Jordan, and that may have been the reason why he was not keen to fight for the possession of Manasseh's inheritance on the west of Jordan.

We see that their failure was due not so much to a lack of strength but of will power. We read that "it came to pass, when the children of Israel were waxen strong, that they put the Canaanites to tribute; but they did not utterly drive them out" (v. 13). That makes sad reading indeed. When they had grown strong enough to have expelled their foes, they still allowed them to dwell among them, merely requiring tribute of them. So once again we see how easily victory may be sacrificed for tribute, and how we take second best when we might have the best.

A STRENGTH NOT OUR OWN

In the closing verses of chapter 17 we see the tribes of Ephraim and Manasseh joining together as "the children of Joseph" to complain to Joshua because, as they said, they had been given one lot and one portion to inherit. This sounds rather strange in view of the fact that Ephraim and Manasseh had been given separate portions, as we have seen. But here they speak as one great tribe which the Lord had blessed hitherto (v. 14).

They might have thought, since Josuha was a member of the tribe of Ephraim, that he would show them special consideration. Instead, he said, "If thou be a great people, then get thee up to the wood country, and cut down for thyself there in the land of the Perizzites and of the giants, if mount Ephraim be too narrow for thee" (v. 15).

But the children of Joseph had evidently surveyed the situation. They knew something of the military strength of the Canaanites. Apparently that led Joshua to concede their claim, for he said, "Thou art a great people, and hast great power: thou shalt not have one lot only: but the mountain shall be thine; for it is a wood, and thou shalt cut it down: and the outgoings of it shall be thine: for thou shalt drive out the Canaanites, though they have iron chariots, and though they be strong" (vv. 17-18).

Joshua not only admitted that they were a great people but he also conceded that they had great power. They probably did not realize how strong they really were. When One mightier than ourselves takes up His abode within us, then we are strong indeed. Whether or not Joshua had something like this in mind we are not told. But the fact that he spoke as he did indicates that he knew of a latent power in those tribes that would enable them to drive out the Canaanites even though they had iron chariots and were strong.

The mountain was to be theirs. The forest also was to be theirs, even to its utmost bounds. But they would have to cut it down. The mountain would not be gained without hard labor on their part.

Joshua assured them of victory and its fruits, but not apart from fighting and hard work. We can almost hear Joshua saying, in the words of another great warrior of a later date, "Finally, my brethren, be strong in the Lord, and in the power of his might" (Eph. 6:10). Then in "full assurance of faith" they could go into battle singing, "Thanks be to God, which giveth us the victory through our Lord Jesus Christ" (I Cor. 15:57).

We must not close this chapter without taking note of other Scriptures which mention the portion of Joseph. When Israel was dying, he said to Joseph, "Behold, I die: but God shall be with you, and bring you again into the land of your fathers. Moreover I have given to thee one portion above thy brethren, which I *took* out of the hand of the Amorite with my sword and with my bow" (Gen. 48:21-22).

Earlier we read that "he *bought* a parcel of a field, where he had spread his tent, at the hand of the children of Hamor, Shechem's father, for an hundred pieces of money. And there he erected an altar, and called it El-elohe-Israel" (Gen. 33:19-20).

One commentator reconciles these passages by saying that "it is . . . probable that the Amorites (Canaanites) having seized upon it during one of his frequent absences, the patriarch, with the united forces of his tribe, recovered it from them by his sword and by his bow. It was now bestowed as a special gift upon Joseph; and *Keil* thinks that the burial of Joseph's bones there (Joshua 24:32) was in consequence of this presentation (Acts 7:16)" (Robert Jamieson).

It was at this place that our Lord met the woman of Samaria (John 4:5) and gave her to drink of the living water which became in her a spring of water "springing up into everlasting life." In that we can see how "Joseph is a fruitful bough, even a fruitful bough by a well; whose branches run over the wall" (Gen. 49:22).

And the end is not yet, for the blessings of Israel, which have prevailed above the blessings of his progenitors unto the utmost bound of the everlasting hills, "shall be on the head of Joseph, and on the crown of the head of him that was separate from his brethren" (v. 26).

CHAPTER THIRTEEN

The Division of the Land Completed

(Joshua 18 and 19)

THE OPENING VERSE of our present portion marks an important point in the history of Israel. Hitherto they had the ark as a center, and Gilgal was the place to which they returned from time to time as their base of operations. Joshua had also built an altar on Mount Ebal upon whose stones he wrote a copy of the law of Moses (Joshua 8). There they offered their burnt offerings and sacrificed their peace offerings to the Lord. "The ark of the covenant" occupied a prominent place on that occasion. But we do not read that the tabernacle was set up at that time.

The setting up of the tabernacle was an indication that things had reached the point where it was possible for the nation as a whole to carry on regular religious services. The military operations incident to the conquest of the land would scarcely have permitted that. But now "the land was subdued before them." Very appropriately, therefore, the tabernacle was set up in Shiloh, which means "peace." Later, of course, Jerusalem became the more permanent center.

Even though they had subdued the land, all had not yet received their inheritance in it. "There remained among the children of Israel seven tribes, which had not yet received their inheritance" (18:

2). In other words, more than half of the tribes had not yet taken possession of that which was theirs. Apparently some had become indifferent, for Joshua said unto the children of Israel, "How long are ye *slack* to go to possess the land, which the LORD God of your fathers hath given you?"

The fact that he addressed himself to "the children of Israel" sounds as though he was speaking to the whole nation. If so, it would indicate that what concerned the seven tribes was something which should concern the whole nation. In that connection it may be of interest to notice that when Paul stood before Agrippa he spoke of "our twelve tribes, instantly serving God day and night" (Acts 26:7). And James addressed his epistle "to the twelve tribes scattered abroad" (James 1:1). In like manner, when Elijah repaired the altar of the Lord that was broken down, he took twelve stones according to the number of the tribes of Israel, even though the nation was divided at the time. All of these men thought of the Lord's people as a unit. And we should think of the Church in the same way. In spite of the many divisions, there is a unity which abides.

The fact that Israel now had a center of worship did not mean that they were to settle down there and forget about those who had not yet entered into their inheritance. It is well to recall that when they were at Horeb, where the tabernacle was erected for the first time, they had to be urged forward. The Lord said, "Ye have dwelt long enough in this mount: turn you, and take your journey" (Deut. 1:6-7). In like manner, Joshua had to stir them up at this time.

In order to give fresh impetus to the project, he commanded them to choose three men from each tribe to go through the land again to describe it and to divide it into seven parts. If each of the twelve tribes had to provide three men, there would be thirty-six men altogether. If only the seven tribes which had not yet inherited are meant here, then there would be twenty-one men in the party. But even that number would be nearly twice the number of those who composed the first expedition which set out from Kadesh-barnea.

Some may wonder about the need for these repeated expeditions. No doubt details would be discovered that had not been noticed before. In the first place, there were more eyes to see them. Next, these men could look around with more deliberation that those who came as spies who had to work swiftly and secretly. Then too, these were probably younger men to whom all of this territory was new. But their joy in making personal discoveries would not be less because some of their older brethren had seen the same things before. There is a sense in which such an expedition may be likened to our study of God's Word. Many have been over the ground before. But each generation of God's children may have the joy of making fresh discoveries in that which is living and abiding and which, therefore, is never stale.

Once an inheritance had been assigned as determined by the casting of lots, the location was final. Accordingly, Joshua told the people, "Judah shall *abide* in their coast on the south, and the house of Joseph shall *abide* in their coasts on the north" (Joshua 18:5). This would indicate to the seven tribes that they were not to look for their inheritance there.

It is true that Simeon, who was one of the seven mentioned here, did inherit "within the inheritance of the children of Judah," but that was because "the portion of the children of Judah was too great for them" (19:9). As for the Levites, Joshua repeated that they were to have "no part" among their brethren. Their inheritances were of a different character altogether, as we have seen in our study of chapter 13. And the tribes of Gad and Reuben, and the half tribe of Manasseh, who had received their inheritance "beyond Jordan on the east," could not seek another portion now on the west.

All of this, of course, is negative. But it has its positive side also. The tribes which had already taken possession must now encourage the others to go and do likewise. And so "the men arose, and went away: and Joshua charged them that went to describe the land, saying, "Go and walk through the land, and describe it, and come again to me, that I may cast lots for you before the LORD in Shiloh" (v. 8).

To really *know* a country one has to *walk* through it and *describe* it. He may fly over it and get a comprehensive view, or he may drive through it and get a passing view. But to really know it he has to walk through it, and then to write down what he has seen. Would to God that we knew more about this in connection with our spiritual heritage. "Eye hath not seen, nor ear heard, neither have entered into the heart of man, the things which God hath prepared for them that love him. But God hath revealed them to us by his spirit: for the Spirit searcheth all things, yea, the deep things of God" (I Cor. 2:9-10). Alas, too many of us are *slack* to possess our possessions.

ALL SATISFIED WITH THEIR PORTIONS

Having walked through the land, and having described it, the men returned to Joshua, and "to the host at Shiloh." The next step was to "rightly divide" what they had explored. In order to do that they must see, first of all, the mind of the Lord.

In this case that was done by casting lots. Since we read of no objection to this method, we conclude that it was satisfactory to all concerned. There is no hint here that some thought that they had been slighted while others were favored.

Judah's portion, the first to be assigned west of the Jordan, contained some of the least desirable parts of the land, such as the wilderness by the Dead Sea. Benjamin and Joseph, on the other hand, had some of the more desirable parts of the land within their borders. But we do not hear of Simeon claiming what belonged to Benjamin, nor of Zebulun demanding part of Issachar's inheritance. The children of Judah might dwell at Jerusalem (Joshua 15:63), but the city itself belonged to the tribe of Benjamin (18:19). Thus it could be said of them as it is said of the Church, "All these worketh that one and the selfsame Spirit, dividing to every man severally as he will (I Cor. 12:11).

The tribe of Benjamin was the first of the seven tribes to have its inheritance assigned. We are told that "their lot came forth between the children of Judah and the children of Joseph" (18:11). Their territory is described, first of all, with respect to its borders, and then with respect to the cities which it included. Among the latter were some of the strongholds of paganism. It is interesting to note that at least three of the places were renamed, perhaps on that very account. In verse 13 mention is made of "Luz, which is Bethel." If this is the place referred to in Genesis 28:19, and there is good reason to believe that it is, then we know that it was Jacob who gave it its new name. To him it was "the house of God" and "the gate of heaven" (Gen. 28:17). That was why he called it Bethel.

Similar changes are recorded in chapter 14, such as "Kirjath-sannah, which is Debir"; "Kirjath-arba,

which is Hebron," and "Kirjath-Baal, which is
Kirjath-jearim" (19:49, 54, 60). Finally, we read of
"Jebusi, which is Jerusalem" (18:28). Such changes
are not without significance, and it is not difficult
to see how they may illustrate changes that are
wrought for believers after they come to know Jesus
Christ as Lord and Saviour. "If any man be in
Christ, he is a new creature: old things are passed
away; behold, all things are become new" (II Cor.
5:17).

"And the second lot came forth to Simeon, even
for the tribe of the children of Simeon according
to their families: and their inheritance was within
the inheritance of the children of Judah" (19:1).
The reason for this is given in verse 9. Simeon was
Judah's older brother and both were sons of Leah,
the older wife of Jacob.

Nothing is said about the borders of Simeon's
inheritance. There was no need for that. But it is
interesting to note that the first place mentioned
among the cities alloted to them was Beer-sheba,
and the last to be mentioned was Baalath-beer, the
Ramah of the south. The word *be'er* (in the original) means "a well." It was Abraham who dug the
well at Beer-sheba, and it was he who gave it that
name (Gen. 21:30-31). It is mentioned quite frequently in the Old Testament. Abraham planted a
grove there "and called there on the name of the
LORD, the everlasting God" (v. 33). It was a sacred
spot to him. Geographically it marked the southern
limit of the land, although theoretically that extended to "the river of Egypt." But primarily it was
a place to which men and beasts came to quench
their thirst. The inheritance of Simeon included two
such places, but Baalath-beer is not so well known
as Beer-sheba.

In the New Testament it is Christ who offers to

quench our thirst (John 4:14, 7:37). And from I Corinthians 10:4 we learn that it was He who did the same for His ancient people as they crossed the desert en route to the promised land. Among all the cities which Simeon inherited, Beer-sheba is outstanding.

Zebulun and Issachar came next in the distribution according to lot, in the third and fourth places respectively. They were also sons of Leah, and once again the older follows the younger, an order we have already noticed in connection with Ephraim and Manasseh. Then the sixth and seventh lots came out for the children of Naphtali and the children of Dan, both sons of Bilhah, Rachel's maid. Once more the natural order is reversed, and the older follows the younger. The spiritual lesson which this teaches bears repeating because it takes some of us a long time to learn.

LAND ENOUGH FOR EVERY TRIBE

"And the seventh lot came out for the children of Dan according to their families" (19:40). The expression, "according to their families," occurs frequently in this book of Joshua, and in the Pentateuch as well. In Exodus 12:21 we find it used in connection with the Passover, when "Moses called for all the elders of Israel, and said unto them, Draw out now and take you a lamb *according to your families,* and kill the passover." In redeeming His people the Lord never had less than the family in mind. We have already had a good illustration of that in connection with Rahab and her household. The matter of the inheritance, too, was to be according to their families. In these days of broken homes and divided families, we do well to ponder this and to pray that our families may share with us the blessings of salvation through Christ our Passover

(I Cor. 5:7) and to participate with us in the "inheritance incorruptible, and undefiled, and that fadeth not away" (I Peter 1:4).

The children of Dan had to fight for possession of their inheritance. "The Amorites forced the children of Dan into the mountain: for they would not suffer them to come down to the valley" (Judges 1:34). Nevertheless, they "went up to fight against Leshem, and took it, and smote it with the edge of the sword, and possessed it, and dwelt therein, and called Leshem, Dan, after the name of Dan their father" (Joshua 19:47). The manner in which the Spirit of God multiplies details here would indicate that something is to be learned from the steps which led up to the capture of the city, and from the change of its name as well.

It appears that the inhabitants of Leshem would not yield to the Israelites without a fight. They may have thought that because some of the Canaanites were not driven out, they too would be left in possession. But it was not to be so in this case. They could not stand before the tribe of Dan, whose name means "judge." And since this is the last battle of which we have record in the book of Joshua, it may be that we have here a type of that "last enemy" that shall be destroyed (I Cor. 15:26) when "the Judge of all the earth" rises up to execute judgment.

"When they had made an end of dividing the land . . . , the children of Israel gave an inheritance to Joshua the son of Nun among them" (Joshua 19:49). He who had been used of God to secure the inheritance for others finally received his own. His willingness to wait for his part is a mark of genuine greatness. The fact that he had to wait until the end does not mean that what he received was inferior, nor just what was left over. It is common practice nowadays to award the highest honors at

the close of a program. We like to think that that
was the case here, even though his distinguished
colleague Caleb was among the earliest to inherit.

Some important and instructive things should be
noted in connection with the inheritance of Joshua.
First, it is spoken of as a gift from the children of
Israel. Second, it was an inheritance "among them,"
and thus suggestive of fellowship. He was not to be
isolated or detached. Then too, it was the place for
which he himself had asked. In giving it to him, they
were not only granting his desire but they were ful-
filling the will of God. It was "according to the word
of the Lord that they gave him the city which he
asked" (v. 50).

The place had two names. According to Gesenius,
Timnath-serah means "abundant portion." In Judges
2:9 it is called Timnath-heres, which, according to
the same authority, means "portion of the sun" or
"sun portion." "Serah" simply reverses the order of
the letters in "Heres." Since the latter is used in connection with the burial of Joshua we can see real
beauty in the change. When his remains were laid
away in the place of his own choosing they were not
laid away in gloom and despair. His burial was the
glorious close of a career which was like "the shining
light, that shineth more and more unto the perfect
day" (Prov. 4:18).

Before his death Joshua built the city and dwelt
in it. He was not only a warrior but also a builder.
No wonder, then, that his earthly career ended in
the "sun portion." How few fighters there are who
are also builders! In Joshua we see that rare combination. May his tribe increase!

CHAPTER FOURTEEN

The Cities of Refuge

(Joshua 20 and 21)

THE DIVINE SOLICITUDE for the safety of the man-slayer, as set forth in Joshua 20 and 21, is a matter of deepest interest. It presents quite a contrast to all of the war and bloodshed we have been occupied with in the preceding chapters. In all of that the Israelites were but instruments in the hands of a righteous and holy God. The iniquity and immorality of the Canaanites was notorious. They had defiled the land to such a degree that it actually vomited them out (Lev. 18:25). They had despised the riches of God's "goodness and forbearance and long-suffering" (Rom. 2:4). Therefore they had to be expelled.

Now we know that constant occupation with such matters is apt to make human life appear very cheap. The terrible increase in the number of murders committed in our country since the two world wars seems to bear that out. But the cinema and television are even more to blame for the way in which the taking of human life is kept before the viewer day after day till even children become hardened to it. But the Scripture here has to do with the manslayer himself.

Before the work of exterminating the Canaanites had begun, while Israel was still in the desert, the Lord commanded Moses to set aside six cities of refuge, "that whosoever killeth any person unawares might flee thither." Such a person was to have the opportunity to present his case to the congregation, and he was to be granted a place of safety where the avenger of blood might not pursue him. There were to be six such cities—three on the east of Jordan and three on the west in the land of Canaan (Num. 35:14)—evenly distributed so as to be readily accessible.

AN ILLUSTRATION OF SALVATION

These things have been used many times to illustrate the gospel as we preach it today. This is especially appropriate in connection with the nation of Israel. It was Peter who said, "Ye men of Israel, . . . ye . . . killed the Prince of life." But he also added, "I wot that through ignorance ye did it, as did also your rulers" (Acts 3:12-17). They did it, as Paul said of himself, "ignorantly in unbelief" (I Tim. 1:13). And we recall that the very One whom they crucified prayed for them, saying, "Father, forgive them; for they know not what they do" (Luke 23:34).

On the other hand, according to a parable spoken by our Lord, there is a sense in which the men of Israel were willful murderers. It was when they recognized Him as the Son of God and His Heir that they said, "This is the heir; come, let us kill him, and seize on his inheritance. And they caught him, and cast him out of the vineyard, and slew him" (Matt. 21:38-39). They would not have that Man to reign over them (Luke 19:14). Therefore "the wrath is come upon them to the uttermost" (I Thess. 2:16). And their city was burned (Matt. 22:7), and they themselves scattered abroad.

Nevertheless, in common with the Gentile, the Jew has enjoyed a day of grace. Thus we can see in the cities of refuge that which is both historical and

prophetic. But this was not their idea; it originated
with God Himself. Truly, He is "the God of all
grace." These cities were not only for the children
of Israel but also "for the stranger that sojourneth
among them, that *whosoever* killeth any person at
unawares might flee thither, and not die by the hand
of the avenger of blood, until he stood before the
congregation" (Joshua 20:9).

The cities of refuge in the land itself were all connected with mountains, and they are said to be "appointed," or "hallowed." Thus we may think of
them as representing the divine, or heavenly, side
of salvation. They seem to be distinguished in this
way from the three cities on the east of Jordan which
are said to be "assigned," or "given." We do not
read of mountains in connection with them. They
may represent the human, or earthly, side of God's
great plan of redemption, wrought out by Him who
is both Son of God and Son of man. No doubt there
is much to be learned from the meanings of the
names of these cities. But we leave that for the
reader to investigate for himself.

OUR SURE REFUGE

In Hebrews 6:18-20 there is, we believe, a reference to all this, but it is by way of contrast rather
than by way of analogy. That, of course, is in keeping with much else that is set forth in the epistle
to the Hebrews. The manslayer, in olden times,
might flee to a city of refuge, and be admitted there,
but his being allowed to remain would depend on the
judgment of the congregation (Num. 35:24). Moreover, if the manslayer were allowed to remain, his
continued safety would depend on his abiding in the
city. If the avenger of blood were to find him
outside the gates of the city at any time, he would
be put to death.

We get an illustration of that in the case of Abner, the son of Ner, who was slain at the gate of Hebron by Joab for the death of Joab's brother Asahel (II Sam. 3:27). And Ahab was slain at Ramoth-gilead, another city of refuge (I Kings 22). That evidently was the judgment of God upon him for the murder of Naboth. In referring to these cases, we are not passing on the merits of either, we are merely using them as illustrations.

Another point to be noticed is the fact that the refuge could not return home until the death of the high priest who happened to be in office at that time. If that high priest were to outlive him, he would never get home; he would be an exile the rest of his days. One can see no "strong consolation" in that.

By way of contrast, we who were once the children of wrath, even as others, have fled for refuge not to some earthly city but "to lay hold upon the hope set before us: which hope we have as an anchor of the soul, both sure and stedfast" (Heb. 6:18-19). Our High Priest has died and risen again. He has met all the claims of divine righteousness and holiness. And now we who believe in Him have peace with God through Him. By so much is the substance better than the shadow. The cities of refuge were but a shadow of good things to come. But in Christ we have "the very image."

THE CITIES OF THE LEVITES

The cities of refuge are mentioned again in Joshua 21 as cities which were given to the Levites, but in every case save one (v. 36) they are still referred to as cities of refuge. According to the sacred record, the request for these cities was very similar to that of the daughters of Zelophehad. The Levites appealed to "Eleazar the priest, and unto Joshua the son of Nun, and unto the heads of the tribes of

Israel" (v. 1), reminding them that a commandment
had been given concerning these cities.

We note that the response to this request was immediate; there was no hesitancy whatever. "The children of Israel gave unto the Levites out of their
inheritance, at the commandment of the LORD, these
cities and their suburbs" (v. 3). This giving "out
of their inheritance" is in keeping with the principle laid down elsewhere in the Word of God, that
those who minister to us in divine things are to
share our material things (I Cor. 9:11). The Lord
has ordained that those who preach the gospel
"should live of the gospel" (v. 14).

The distribution of the Levites among the tribes
of Israel seems to have been for the purpose of
facilitating their ministry to all. In this we see the
very opposite of the centralization of ecclesiastical
power. In that connection it should be noted that
Jerusalem was not among the cities given to the
Levites. Among the cities which are mentioned by
name, Hebron takes the first place.

Earlier that city was given to Caleb. But here
we find that he had only "the fields of the city,
and the villages thereof" (v. 12). Since we read of
no objection to this, we assume that he willingly
yielded the city itself to the Levites. Thus, by in-
ference, we learn something more of the character
and greatness of Caleb.

The fact that there were exactly forty-eight cities
given to the Levites is also significant, we believe.
This is just double the number of the courses into
which David divided the priesthood (I Chron. 24).
These cities were situated on both sides of the Jordan, and thus, like the cities of refuge which were
numbered among them, they were naturally divided
into two groups. It may be that we have here a
suggestion of the twofold ministry of the priests.

Scripture teaches us that our priesthood, as believers, is both "an holy priesthood" and "a royal priesthood" (I Peter 2:5, 9).

We get a similar combination in Hebrews 5:1-2, where it is stated that the high priest was to "offer both gifts and sacrifices for sins" and to "have compassion on the ignorant, and on them that are out of the way." The one was Godward, and the other manward. In this way a beautiful balance would be maintained.

Even though the cities of the Levites were naturally divided into two groups by the Jordan, we find that the children of Gershon and the children of Merari were given cities on both sides of the river (vv. 6-7). If, as we have suggested, the one side may be used to represent the heavenly side of things, and the other the earthly side, then we have here an illustration of the balance that should exist between our services for the Lord, whether they be in the sanctuary or on the street. We are apt to divide our work and call one part sacred and the other secular. Actually these are two sides of the same thing. Whatever we do, we should do it heartily as unto the Lord.

The chapter closes with a precious reference to the faithfulness of God. He had sworn to the fathers of Israel that He would give them the land. And He "gave unto Israel *all* the land which he sware to give unto their fathers." Moreover, He "delivered *all* their enemies into their hand. There failed not ought of any good thing which the Lord had spoken unto the house of Israel; *all* came to pass."

> Lord, 'tis enough, we ask no more;
>   Thy grace around us pours
> Its rich and unexhausted store
>   And all its joy is ours.

CHAPTER FIFTEEN

The Altar of Witness

(Joshua 22)

THE RETURN of the <u>forty thousand men</u> of Reuben,
Gad, and Manasseh (Josuha 4:13) to their homes in
Gilead was a sign, so to speak, that the conquest
of Canaan was actually complete. Joshua com-
mended them highly as he dismissed them. They had
been obedient soldiers (22:2), faithful to their
brethren and, above all, they had kept the charge
of the commandment of Jehovah their God (v. 3).
They merited, and received an honorable discharge.

But Joshua was wise enough to know that the
enemy of souls would spoil all of this if he could.
Therefore he exhorted them to "take diligent heed
to do the commandment and the law" which Moses,
the servant of Jehovah, had commanded, and to *love*
the Lord their God, and to *walk* in all His ways, and
to *keep* His commandments, and to *cleave* unto Him,
and to *serve* Him with all their hearts and all their
souls. Then he blessed them and sent them away.

"Love . . . walk . . . keep . . . cleave . . . serve."
Five weighty words! The whole speech was brief.
As an example of brevity, and yet of completeness,
it is a worthy farewell from a great general to his
soldiers. Twice it is recorded that he blessed them
(vv. 6-7). And they were well laden with material
blessings also: with cattle, silver, gold, bronze, iron,

and much clothing. It was the spoil of their enemies, and Joshua exhorted them to divide it with their brethren (v. 8).

About half a century before this their fathers had "spoiled the Egyptians." When the Israelites "spoiled the Egyptians," they were, in effect, collecting the wages which they had earned as slaves. The spoiling of the Canaanites may be justified by the fact that those who had accumulated all this wealth had proved themselves unworthy of it. They failed to acknowledge Him who alone could say, "Every beast of the forest is mine, and the cattle upon a thousand hills. . . . for the world is mine, and the fulness thereof" (Ps. 50:10, 12).

AN OFFERING OF PRAISE FOR VICTORY

It is very gratifying to read that those who had been the recipients of such bounty did not forget the One who had given them the victory and who had enriched them with the spoils of victory. Accordingly, they built "an altar by Jordan, a great altar to see to" (22:10).

The building of such a monument was not without precedent. Jacob built such a memorial and called it Galeed, a name which, by the way, includes the very name, Ed, given to this altar. But when the news of this reached their brethren there was great consternation among them. "The children of Israel heard say, . . . " (v. 11). One wonders who brought the news, and with what tone of voice. How often news is brought which may be true enough so far as the wording of it is concerned, but the tone of voice in which it is delivered may completely mislead those who hear it.

Such may have been the case here. As a result, "the whole congregation of the children of Israel

gathered themselves together at Shiloh" to go to
war against their brethren (v. 12). But before they
actually went to war, calmer counsel prevailed and
it was decided to send "Phinehas, the son of Eleazar
the priest, and with him ten princes" (vv. 13-14) to
the two and a half tribes, with a message which
stands out in dark contrast to the farewell speech
and double benediction with which Joshua had dismissed them.

With a great show of authority they declared,
"Thus saith the whole congregation of the LORD"
(v. 16), and forthwith the building of the altar at
the Jordan was branded as a trespass and rebellion
against the Lord. They actually accused their brethren of turning from the Lord (v. 16), and likened
their act to "the iniquity of Peor" and the trespass
of Achan. Instead of allowing their brethren to present their reasons for building the altar, they virtually
accused them of apostasy.

This might easily have led to a rupture that in
time nothing could have healed. But we have to ad-
mire the spirit of the accused as they listened to the
charges being brought against them by those with
whom, and for whom, they had fought so valiantly
all those years.

It might have been better to have consulted with
their brethren before building the altar. But when
one has the impulse to do something like this, he
does not always stop to think how his decision may
be viewed by others. It is those who have ulterior
motives who are usually wise enough to anticipate
objections and to forestall them, if possible. The
naïveté with which all was done, for there was nothing secret or surreptitious about it, should have made
Phinehas and the ten princes slow to bring such
awful charges against their brethren.

THE DEFENSE

The defense which the accused made is very beautiful. They did not begin by saying, "Thus saith the whole congregation of Reuben, Gad, and Manasseh." Their answer began with, "The LORD God of gods, the LORD God of gods, he knoweth, and Israel he shall know; if it be in rebellion, or if in transgression against the LORD" (v. 22). They were willing to be destroyed if such were the case. "Save us not this day." "Let the LORD himself require it; . . . if we have not rather done it for fear of this thing, saying, In time to come your children might speak unto our children, saying, What have ye to do with the LORD God of Israel? . . . Ye have no part in the LORD" (vv. 24-25). They anticipated the day when those living on the west of Jordan might look down on those living east of it, as though the unity of God's people were determined by physical boundaries. It is not boundaries that unify, but a Divine Center—Christ Himself—who makes His people one.

The land to the east of the Jordan was just as much a gift from Jehovah as the land which lay to the west of it. It was He who provided the land with three cities of refuge on either side. Then, too, the Levites were assigned, as we have seen, to the cities on the east as well as on the west. In either case it was "the land of their possession, whereof they were possessed according to the word of the LORD by the hand of Moses" (v. 9). Therefore the insinuation that the land might be unclean (v. 19) was quite uncalled for. Today, in like manner, we may go too far in hasty judgment of brethren who do not happen to live on our side of the river.

The fact that the explanation offered by these brethren was good in the sight of Phinehas and the ten princes with him (v. 30) leads one to wonder why there was not one word of apology for the hasty judgment pronounced in the first place. But when word was brought back to the whole assembly, the thing "pleased the children of Israel," and they blessed God. Nothing further was said about going up "to destroy the land wherein the children of Reuben and Gad dwelt" (v. 33). But we fail to find any expression of regret for what they had said before. That may account for the apathy displayed by Reuben later, and "the divisions of Reuben" for which "there were great searchings of heart" (Judges 5:15-16).

In any case, there stood the altar, not as a symbol of independence and rebellion but as "a witness between us that the LORD is God" (v. 34). So far as the record goes, it never served any other purpose. If there was defection later, this altar was not the cause of it. We should take the statement of its builders at face value and credit them with sincerity in erecting it.

We all need such an attitude, and we need to remember that our Lord said, "He that is not against us is on our part" (Mark 9:40). Even that is something for which to be thankful in times like these.

CHAPTER SIXTEEN

Joshua's Valedictories

(Joshua 23 and 24)

IT IS QUITE REMARKABLE that neither Joshua nor Eleazar appear to have had any active part in the trouble which arose over the building of the altar at the Jordan. Phinehas, the son of Eleazar, seems to have been the leader in that unhappy affair. But we see in these chapters that it was Joshua who called all Israel together for a final word. Whether or not these two chapters deal with two separate gatherings is a moot question. It is quite possible that they have to do with one general event, but that all that is recorded did not take place the same day.

The last time the nation was gathered together as a whole was at Shiloh (chapter 18). Then there were still seven tribes which had not taken possession of their inheritances. Now all were settled, and Jehovah had given them rest from all of their enemies. Joshua, faithful old warrior that he was, had fulfilled his commission and was about to go the way of all the earth.

Very humbly he recounted what the Lord had done for them, how He had fought for them, and how He had promised that He would expel and dispossess the nations that remained. But His continued favor depended on their continued obedience to His word, and their separation from the Canaanites. In view of all that the Lord had done for them, these conditions were not unreasonable.

Joshua credited the people with having cleaved to the Lord unto that day (v. 8). In fact, we do not find here one word of censure or adverse criticism; all is commendatory. But he warned them that they would have to persevere in this. If not, they would discover to their sorrow that God would not drive out the remaining Canaanites from before them, but that they would be as snares and traps unto them, scourges in their sides, and thorns in their eyes; and they themselves would perish from off the good land which the Lord their God had given them (v. 13).

"Snares . . . traps . . . scourges . . . thorns"! Such is the divine description of the wicked nations which the Lord would use to discipline His people if necessary, just as He used Satan to sift Peter as wheat. Paul's thorn in the flesh is also called "the messenger of Satan" (II Cor. 12:7). So we see how the Lord may use even Satan in the discipline of His people.

But God is just as loving in His government as He is in His grace. In all of His ways, as well as in His acts (Ps. 103:7), He is consistent with His holiness and righteousness. He who expels nations because of their wickedness will not tolerate wickedness in His own people. And the fact that the people apparently accepted this shows that it seemed right to them. Every true child of God will admit that God's warnings are just as loving as His commendations. He loves us too well to let us go unwarned into that which would bring sorrow and regret later.

Summing up what we have here, we note three things. The first of these is the exhortation to *obey* (v. 6). The second is the command to *cleave* unto the Lord (v. 8). And finally, "Take good heed therefore unto yourselves, that ye *love* the Lord your God" (v. 11). One may obey another without cleaving to him. Again, one might cleave to another for selfish reasons, without really loving him. But the kind of obedience God expects, and deserves, is that which comes from the heart.

It has been noted by others that what we have here is very similar to the valedictory of Moses, recorded in the book of Deuteronomy, and not unlike the words of Paul as recorded in Acts 20 and elsewhere in his epistles. These men saw days of declension ahead and warned their brethren beforehand. In like manner Joshua prophesied of Israel's lapse into idolatry, and the Lord's judgment upon them because of it (vv. 15-16).

JOSHUA'S LAST WORD TO ISRAEL

The last chapter of our book gives details not found in chapter 23. In the first place we are told that this gathering took place in Shechem, which was centrally located so that none would have to travel very far to get to it. It was a city of refuge in the hill country not far from Joshua's own home. Second, we read that the people "presented themselves before God." They were not there merely to hear about God but to be made aware of His presence. Third, we note that Joshua opened his address with the solemn formula, "Thus saith the LORD God of Israel" (v. 2).

In the preceding chapter Joshua spoke of what Jehovah had done for them, that is, for the generation then living, and of what their attitude was to be toward the Canaanites which still remained in the land. Some reference was made to the gods of those nations but it was more or less incidental. In this chapter he deals at some length with the subject of idolatry.

He began by reminding them that their ancestors were idolaters when they lived beyond the Euphates

river, here referred to as "the flood" (v. 3). He
actually named Terah, Abraham, and Nahor. It
would appear from a statement made by Laban to
Jacob that all three of these later became worshipers
of the true God (Gen. 31:53). But Abraham
was the only one of the three who completely separated himself in obedience to the call of God. Of
him the Lord said, through Joshua, "I took your
father Abraham from the other side of the flood
[river], and led him throughout all the land of
Canaan, and multiplied his seed, and gave him
Isaac" (v. 3).

There is much food for thought in that verse. The
reference to the *taking* of Abraham is very striking.
In Hebrews 11:8 we read that "he went out," but
here God says, "I took him out." In Genesis 12:6
we read, "Abram passed through the land," but
here God says, "I led him throughout the land." It
was the Lord who multiplied his seed, and gave him
Isaac. But there was a time when Abraham thought
that Ishmael was the fulfillment of God's promise
to him. In this passage the divine side of these things
is emphasized.

This is continued as we proceed into the next
stage of Israel's history. It was the Lord who sent
Moses and Aaron to them; it was He who plagued
Egypt; it was He who brought Israel out of Egypt;
and it was He who brought them into the land of
Canaan. The whole of the wilderness journey is referred to in eight words: "Ye dwelt in the wilderness
a long season." There are only four words in the
original. Nothing whatever is said about the memor-
able battle with Amalek in which Joshua distinguished himself. Joshua's purpose was to magnify
the Lord, not himself. Like Paul he could say, "Not
I, but Christ."

Yes, it was the Lord who destroyed their enemies

(v. 8), and it was He who caused Balaam to bless the Israelites after he had been hired by Balak to curse them. It was He who delivered the Canaanites into their hands, and gave them their land. As a result, they were living in cities which they did not build, and they were eating of vineyards and olive-yards which they did not plant (v. 13). On the basis of all this, Joshua exhorted them to "fear the LORD, and serve him in sincerity and in truth," and to put away the strange gods which their fathers served on the other side of the Euphrates, and also in Egypt (v. 14).

ISRAEL'S BESETTING SIN

Idolatry seems to have been one of Israel's besetting sins. Their earliest ancestors served other gods, as we have seen. When Jacob and his family left Laban, Rachel carried off her father's gods (Gen. 31:30-34). And when they arrived in the land Jacob ordered his household to put away these "strange gods," and he hid them under an oak tree that was by Shechem (Gen. 35:2, 4). It was in that same place that Joshua urged his generation to put away the gods which their fathers served (v. 14). They not only clung to the gods of their forefathers, but it seems that they brought Egyptian idols with them also.

When Joshua said to them, "Choose you this day whom ye will serve," he was not asking them to make a choice between the true God and these idols. What he said was; "If it seem evil unto you to serve the LORD, choose you this day whom ye will serve; whether the gods which your fathers served . . . or the gods of the Amorites" (v. 15). If they wanted to be idolaters, it would make no difference whether they served Mesopotamian gods or Amorite gods. An idol is nothing anyhow (I Cor. 8:4). As for

Joshua, he would have neither of these. He and his
house would serve the Lord. Happy is the man that
can speak in this way, not only for himself but for
his family as well.

Apparently the people were ready to follow him
in this. They freely owned that it was the Lord who
had done all for them, and they said "Therefore
will we also serve the LORD; for he is our God"
(v. 18).

The influence of Joshua was felt for more than
a generation. "The people served the LORD all the
days of Joshua, and all the days of the elders that
outlived Joshua" (Judges 2:7). The reading of these
words makes us covet the honor of exerting an influence like that!

A monument was duly erected to commemorate
this solemn occasion "by the sanctuary of the LORD"
(v. 26). Thus they would be reminded of what they
had promised every time they gathered there. "So
Joshua let the people depart, every man to his inheritance" (v. 28).

Like his great predecessor, Moses, Joshua ended
his earthly career with honor. The book which bears
his name records no moral blemish on his name. He
may be blamed by some for not having detected the
sin of Achan before the humbling defeat at Ai. No
doubt he should have made more careful inquiry
before making a covenant with the Gibeonites. But
no one can put his finger on one moral blemish in
his life. He stands out as one of the great men of
other days, and worthy of our imitation. He died at
the age of 110 years. For his day and generation
he was "the servant of the LORD" (v. 29). That title
is often applied to Moses in this book, but this is
the first and only time that it is used of Joshua. He
had "arrived," as we would say.

"They buried him in the border of his inheritance in Timnath-serah, which is in mount Ephraim, on the north side of the hill of Gaash" (v. 30). Since we have already commented on this place and its other name, in our study of chapter 19, not much needs to be added here except to point out that his remains were laid away "on the north side." When the Psalmist described Mount Zion, he spoke of it as "beautiful for situation, the joy of the whole earth, . . . on the sides of the north" (Ps. 48:2). Perhaps this too was beautiful for situation, and so we get this added detail here.

The book closes with brief notices of two other burials. "The bones of Joseph, which the children of Israel brought up out of Egypt, buried they in Shechem, in a parcel of ground which Jacob bought . . . : and it became the inheritance of the children of Joseph" (v. 32).

"And Eleazar the son of Aaron died; and they buried him in a hill that pertained to Phinehas his son, which was given him in mount Ephraim." Thus the Spirit of God brings together three men who stand out in the history of Israel. Joshua was the one who led them into the land and caused them to possess it. Joseph was noted for the fact that he was a great provider who kept a hungry world from starvation in the days of famine. Eleazar, as high priest, would give protection to those who sought asylum in a city of refuge. On the other hand, his death would be the signal for the release of such, so that they might return to their homes.

There is nothing haphazard about these closing verses; they are divinely arranged. And it is lovely indeed to be able to close our meditations on the chord of possession, provision, and protection—a threefold blessing, as it were, from Him who has blessed us with all spiritual blessings in heavenly places in Christ. "Unto him be glory in the church by Christ Jesus throughout all ages, world without end. Amen."